the fruit kitchen

the fruit kitchen

A CELEBRATION OF FRESH AND ZESTY RECIPES

Consulting Editor: Emma Summer

LORENZ BOOKS

This edition first published in 1999 by Lorenz Books

© Anness Publishing Limited 1999

Lorenz Books is an imprint of
Anness Publishing Limited
27 West 20th Street
New York, NY 10011

ISBN 0-7548-0259-0

Publisher: Joanna Lorenz
Senior Cookbook Editor: Linda Fraser
Project Editor: Emma Gray
Jacket Designer: Luise Roberts
Designers: Lilian Lindblom, Bill Mason and Lisa Tai
Illustrations: Anna Koska
Additional Text: Christine Ingram

Photographers: Karl Adamson, Edward Allwright, Steve Baxter, James Duncan, Michelle Garrett, Nelson Hargreaves,
Amanda Heywood, Tim Hill, David Jordan, Don Last, Patrick McLeavey, Michael Michaels, Thomas Odulate.
Recipes: Alex Barker, Carla Capalbo, Kit Chan, Carole Clements, Roz Denny, Nicola Diggins, Rafi Fernandez, Christine France,
Sarah Gates, Shirley Gill, Rosamund Grant, Deh-Ta Hsiung, Patricia Lousada, Norma MacMillan, Sue Maggs, Sallie Morris,
Katherine Richmond, Anne Sheasby, Liz Trigg, Laura Washburn, Pamela Westland, Steven Wheeler, Elizabeth Wolf-Cohen.
Food for photography: Madeleine Brehaut, Joanne Craig, Marilyn Forbes, Hilary Guy, Carole Handslip, Jane Hartshorn, Cara Hobday, Maria Kelly,
Wendy Lee, Blake Minton, Kirsty Rawlings, Jane Stevenson, Fiona Tillett, Judy Williams and Elizabeth Wolf-Cohen.

Printed and bound in Singapore

1 3 5 7 9 10 8 6 4 2

contents

INTRODUCTION

There is nothing like the sight of a glorious display of fruit to lift the spirits and whet the appetite. Glowing colors, aromatic scents and tastes that range from tantalizingly tart to superbly sweet—all these attributes help to make fruit the treat it is. Add the fact that it is a supremely healthy food, bursting with natural, energy-giving sugars, minerals and vitamins, in all the right amounts, and it is easy to understand why fruit plays such a central role in our diet.

When energy levels are low, a few grapes, a banana, apricots or an apple, whether fresh or dried, revitalize us in a few moments. Fruit provides the perfect guilt-free snack, since most varieties are fat-free and contain very few calories. Nearly all fruits have a high proportion of water, which makes them satisfyingly thirst-quenching in hot weather, instead of a drink at any time.

Cooked fruit, on the other hand, is a wonderfully warming and comforting dessert when the days are cold and dreary. No wonder we can't wait for winter to savor satisfying desserts such as Blueberry and Pear Pie and the classic Apple Pie.

Fruit is amazingly versatile. You could easily base an entire meal on it without repeating any colors, textures or flavors. Starting with Thai Chicken and Citrus Soup, you could progress to Venison with Cranberry Sauce, and finish with a flourish by serving fresh Raspberry and Passionfruit Swirls. Fruit and cheese are classic companions, so you could just as easily end a meal with a platter of fine cheeses accompanied by grapes, pears and apples, or dried fruits and nuts.

Fruit is no longer the seasonal produce it once was. Nowadays, thanks to sophisticated transportation methods, all types of fruit from every country are available almost all year round. Travelers who have sampled exotic produce abroad now find it gracing the shelves of their local greengrocer or supermarket, giving them a taste of the tropical climates at home and a chance to experiment with new recipes.

There is nothing to beat the flavor of freshly picked fruit, however; sinking your teeth into a ripe strawberry, or taking a bite out of an apple that only seconds ago was on the tree, are two of life's greatest pleasures, only to be equalled by transforming such superb ingredients into delicious dishes.

PREPARING FRUIT

For some fruits, the only preparation needed is washing or wiping with a damp cloth; others must be peeled, skinned, pitted, stoned or seeded. The skin protects and preserves fruit, so wash and peel it just before using to conserve its freshness.

FIRM FRUIT

PEELING

Some firm fruits, such as apples and pears, can be eaten raw without peeling. For cooking, peeling is often necessary. Pare off the skin as thinly as possible to avoid losing the valuable nutrients under the skin.

Wash the fruit and pat dry using paper towels. Use a small, sharp paring knife or a vegetable peeler to pare off the skin in long, thin vertical strips. Pears are best peeled by this method. For apples, thinly peel all around the fruit in a spiral.

CORING

To core whole apples and pears, place the sharp edge of a corer over the stem end of the fruit. Press down firmly, then twist slightly; the core, complete with seeds, will come out in the center of the corer. Push out the core from the handle end.

SEGMENTING

Halve the fruit lengthwise, then cut into quarters or segments.

Carefully cut out the central core and seeds, with a small sharp knife.

CITRUS FRUIT

PEELING

It is very important to remove all of the bitter white pith that lies just beneath the rind or zest of citrus fruits.

To peel firm-skinned fruits, hold the fruit over a bowl to catch the juice and use a sharp knife to cut off the skin.

For loose-skinned fruit, such as tangerines, pierce the skin with your forefinger at the stalk end and peel off the skin. Pull off all the white shreds adhering to the fruit.

SEGMENTING

Use a small serrated knife to cut down in between the membranes enclosing the segments; cut along both sides and the base of the segment, then carefully ease out the flesh of the fruit.

GRATING

Citrus rind or zest adds a wonderful flavor to many dishes. If it is to be eaten raw, grate it finely, using the fine face of a grater. Remove only the colored zest; if you grate too deeply into the peel, you will be in danger of including the bitter white pith. For cooking, pare off long, thin strips of zest using a zester. These thin strips also make a stylish garnish.

Make sure that you use a whole lemon that has good, firm flesh; soft loose skin will not grate easily. Hold the grater over a bowl, or stand on a board to collect the zest.

SOFT FRUIT

PEELING

Fruits, such as peaches, nectarines and apricots, can be peeled with a sharp paring knife, but this may waste some of the delicious flesh. It is better to loosen the skins by dipping them briefly in boiling water.

Make a tiny nick in the skin. Cover with boiling water and let sit for 15–30 seconds, depending on the ripeness of the fruit. Remove the fruit with a slotted spoon and peel off the skin, which should come off easily.

COOKING FRUIT

There are some fruits that many people wouldn't consider cooking, but most fruit can be cooked in a variety of ways. A few experiments can yield quite delicious results.

GRILLING

Any firm fruits can be grilled, with or without sugar. Tropical fruits, such as pineapple and bananas, are particularly good for grilling. For desserts, they can be cut into 1-inch wedges or chunks and threaded on skewers to make kebabs. Brush the fruit with honey before grilling.

Halve the fruit or cut into pieces, removing the core if necessary. Brush with melted butter and grill under medium heat, turning occasionally, until tender and browned on all sides.

POACHING

Apples and pears, fruits with pits, figs, rhubarb and even grapes can be poached, either whole, halved or in segments. The classic poaching liquid is syrup and usually consists of 1 part sugar boiled with 2 parts water for about 2 minutes or until clear. The syrup can be flavored with lemon, orange or spices, such as cinnamon or vanilla. Red or white wine can also be used.

Bring the poaching liquid to a boil. Lower the heat and add the fruit. Simmer gently until the fruit is just tender.

BAKING

Apples and pears, fruits with pits, such as peaches, nectarines, apricots and plums, as well as figs and rhubarb can be baked whole or in halves, wedges or slices according to type. If you want the fruit to remain very moist, add a few drops of water to the cooking dish and cover with a lid.

Put the fruit in a shallow ovenproof dish, add a little water, and sprinkle with sugar to taste. Top the fruit with small pieces of butter. Bake in a preheated oven at 350°F until tender.

DEEP-FRYING

For fruit fritters, such as pineapple, apple or banana, peel the fruit and cut into chunks or thick slices or, if they are not too large, deep-fry them whole.

Heat oil for deep-frying to 360°F or until a cube of dried bread sizzles when it is added to the pan. Coat the pieces of fruit in batter and deep-fry until the fritters rise to the surface of the hot oil and are golden brown. Drain the fritters on paper towels and sprinkle with sugar.

PUREEING

Fruit can be puréed for sauces, ice creams and sorbets. Some types must be cooked first; others, like berries, can be puréed raw.

For cooked, peeled fruit, mash with a potato masher for a coarse purée. For a finer purée, purée cooked, peeled fruit in a food processor or push through a food mill or sieve or strainer.

For berries, wash briefly and push through a fine nylon sieve or strainer, using the back of a large spoon or ladle. If you prefer, purée the berries in a food processor, then sieve the purée to remove any seeds, skin or stalks.

CARAMELIZING

Fruits glisten and look pretty when caramelized. Small fruits like cherries, black currants and raspberries can be used whole. Larger fruits should be cubed.

Combine scant 1 cup sugar and ¼ cup water in a small heavy saucepan. Stir over low heat until the sugar has dissolved. When the mixture boils, add 1 teaspoon lemon juice and boil until the syrup turns a deep golden brown.

Add 1 tablespoon hot water and shake the pan to mix. Spear a piece of fruit on a fork and dip it into the caramel to coat. Let sit on an oiled baking sheet until the caramel cools and hardens.

appetizers and side dishes

Many sweet and sharp-flavored fruits can be combined

successfully with savory ingredients to make wonderful

first-course dishes that stimulate the appetite for the

meal to come, and side dishes that are the perfect

complement to a main course. The following recipes

marry flavors to great effect, creating an intriguing

range of taste sensations.

THAI CHICKEN AND CITRUS SOUP

An exotic and aromatic soup that combines delicious flavors from South-East Asia.

Serves 4

1 tablespoon vegetable oil

1 garlic clove, finely chopped

*2 boned chicken breasts (about 6 ounces
  each), skinned and chopped*

½ teaspoon ground turmeric

¼ teaspoon hot chili powder

3 ounces coconut cream

3¾ cups hot chicken stock

2 tablespoons lemon juice

2 tablespoons chunky peanut butter

*1 cup thread egg noodles, broken into
  small pieces*

1 tablespoon finely chopped scallions

1 tablespoon chopped fresh cilantro

salt and ground black pepper

*2 tablespoons shredded coconut and ½
  fresh red chili, seeded and finely
  chopped, to garnish*

Heat the oil in a large pan and fry the garlic for 1 minute until lightly golden. Add the chicken, turmeric and chili powder and stir-fry for a further 3–4 minutes.

Crumble the coconut cream into the hot chicken broth and stir until dissolved. Pour on to the chicken and add the lemon juice, peanut butter and egg noodles. Stir well to mix.

Cover the pan and simmer for about 15 minutes. Add the scallions and fresh cilantro, then season well and cook for a further 5 minutes.

Meanwhile, place the coconut and chili in a small frying pan and heat for 2–3 minutes, stirring frequently, until the coconut is lightly browned.

Serve the soup in bowls sprinkled with the fried coconut and chili.

PARSNIP AND APPLE SOUP

A hearty, warming soup that's excellent served on a cold winter's day.

Serves 8–10

4 tablespoons sweet butter

2 large onions, sliced

1 garlic clove, chopped

2 large parsnips, scrubbed and cubed

2 firm, tart cooking apples (about 1 pound), peeled, cored and cubed

2 teaspoons medium curry powder

6¼ cups chicken broth

1¼ cups light cream

salt and ground black pepper

For the topping

2 tablespoons sweet butter

1 cup pecans, chopped

⅔ cup crème fraîche or sour cream

Heat the butter in a large pan and sauté the onions and garlic over moderate heat until the onions are translucent. Stir in the parsnips and apples and sauté for 3 minutes more, stirring occasionally. Add the curry powder and stir to mix. Cook for 1 minute more. Pour on the broth, bring to a boil, cover the pan and simmer for 20 minutes. Remove from the heat and cool slightly. Pour into a food processor or blender and process until smooth. Return the soup to the pan. Stir in the cream and seasoning and heat gently.

To make the topping, heat the butter in a pan and sauté the pecans over moderate heat for 5 minutes. Serve the soup in bowls topped with the crème fraîche or sour cream and sprinkled with the sautéed pecans.

FIG, APPLE, AND DATE SALAD

Sweet Mediterranean figs and dates combine especially well with crisp eating apples.

Serves 4

6 large eating apples

juice of ½ lemon

6 ounces fresh dates

1 ounce white marzipan

1 teaspoon orange flower water

4 tablespoons plain yogurt

4 fresh green or purple figs

4 toasted almonds, to garnish

COOK'S TIP

When buying fresh dates, avoid any that look shriveled. They should be plump and shiny, yellow-red to golden brown and with smooth skins.

Core the apples and slice thinly with a sharp knife. Leave the skins on. Cut into fine matchsticks. Place in a bowl and toss with lemon juice.

Remove the pits from the dates and cut the flesh into fine strips, then combine with the apple slices in the bowl.

In a separate bowl, soften the marzipan with orange flower water and combine with the yogurt. Mix together well until smooth.

Divide the apples and dates among the center of four plates. Remove the stem from each of the figs and divide the fruit into quarters without cutting right through the base. Squeeze the base with the thumb and forefinger of each hand to open up the fruit. Place a fig in the center of each salad, spoon in the yogurt filling, and serve garnished with a toasted almond.

PLANTAIN AND GREEN BANANA SALAD

Cooking plantains and bananas in their skins helps to retain the soft texture so that they absorb all the flavor of the dressing.

Serves 4

2 ripe yellow plantains

3 green bananas

1 garlic clove, crushed

1 red onion

*1–2 tbsp chopped fresh
    cilantro*

3 tbsp sunflower oil

1½ tbsp malt vinegar

salt and coarse-grain black pepper

Slit the plantains and bananas lengthwise along their natural ridges, then cut in half, and place in a large saucepan. Pour in water to cover, add a little salt, and bring to a boil.

Boil the plantains and bananas gently for 20 minutes until tender, then drain well. When they are cool enough to handle, peel and cut them into medium-size slices.

Put the plantain and banana slices into a bowl and add the crushed garlic, turning to mix.

Cut the onion in half and slice it thinly. Add to the bowl with the chopped fresh cilantro, oil, and vinegar. Add salt and pepper to taste. Toss to mix, then serve.

COOK'S TIP

Red onions are mild and sweet, so they are ideal for mixing in salads and for adding extra flavor to sandwiches.

FRESH BERRY SALSA

This bright, tangy salsa is spicy hot – add more jalapeño pepper to make it even spicier. It is good served with broiled chicken or fish.

Makes about 2½ cups

1 fresh jalapeño pepper

½ red onion, minced

2 scallions, chopped

1 tomato, finely diced

1 small yellow bell pepper, seeded and minced

¼ cup chopped fresh cilantro

¼ teaspoon salt

1 tablespoon raspberry vinegar

1 tablespoon fresh orange juice

1 teaspoon honey

1 tablespoon olive oil

1 cup strawberries, hulled

1 cup blueberries or blackberries

1 cup raspberries

Finely mince the jalapeño pepper (discarding the seeds and membrane if a slightly milder flavor to the salsa is desired). Place the pepper in a medium-size bowl.

Add the red onion, scallions, tomato, bell pepper, and cilantro and stir to blend thoroughly.

In a small bowl, whisk together the salt, vinegar, orange juice, honey, and oil. Pour over the jalapeño mixture and stir well.

Coarsely chop the strawberries. Add to the jalapeño mixture with the blueberries or blackberries and raspberries, and stir to blend. Let stand at room temperature 3 hours.

Serve the salsa at room temperature.

SPINACH PLANTAIN ROUNDS

This delectable way of serving plantains is a little effortful to make, but well worth the trouble. The plantains must be ripe, but still firm.

Serves 4

2 large yellow plantains, peeled

oil, for frying

2 tbsp butter

1 tbsp finely chopped onion

2 garlic cloves, crushed

1lb fresh spinach, chopped

pinch of freshly grated nutmeg

1 egg, beaten

whole wheat flour, for dipping

salt and ground black pepper

Using a small sharp knife, carefully cut each plantain lengthwise into four slices. Heat a little oil in a large skillet and fry the slices on both sides until pale gold in color, but not fully cooked. Lift out and drain on paper towels, and reserve the oil in the skillet.

Melt the butter in a saucepan and sauté the onion and garlic for 2–3 minutes until the onion is soft. Add the spinach and nutmeg, with salt and pepper to taste. Cover and cook for about 5 minutes until the spinach has reduced. Cool, then tip into a strainer, and press out any excess moisture.

Curl the plantain slices into rings and secure each ring with a wooden toothpick. Pack each ring with a little of the spinach mixture.

Place the egg and flour in two separate dishes. Add a little more oil to the skillet, if necessary, and heat until moderately hot. Dip the spinach and plantain rounds in the egg, and then in the flour. Fry on both sides for 1–2 minutes until golden brown. Drain on paper towels and serve hot or cold.

COOK'S TIP

If fresh spinach is not available, use frozen spinach. Thaw completely and drain thoroughly in a strainer before cooking.

STEAMED BANANA LEAF PACKETS

Very neat and delicate, these seafood packets from Thailand make an excellent appetizer or light lunch.

Serves 4

8oz crab meat

2oz peeled shrimp, chopped

6 drained water chestnuts, chopped

2 tbsp chopped bamboo shoots

1 tbsp chopped scallion

1 tsp chopped fresh ginger root

2 tbsp soy sauce

1 tbsp fish sauce

12 rice sheets

banana leaves, for lining steamer

oil, for brushing

2 scallions, shredded, 2 fresh red
chilies, seeded and sliced, and
cilantro leaves, to garnish

Combine the crab meat, chopped shrimp, chestnuts, bamboo shoots, scallion, and ginger in a bowl. Mix well, then add 1 tbsp of the soy sauce and all the fish sauce. Stir until blended.

Take a rice sheet and dip it in warm water. Place it on a flat surface and leave for a few seconds to soften.

Place a spoonful of the filling in the center of the sheet and fold into a square packet. Repeat with the rest of the rice sheets and seafood mixture.

Use banana leaves to line a steamer, then brush them with oil. Place the packets, seam side down, on the leaves and steam over a high heat for 6–8 minutes or until the filling is cooked. Transfer to a plate and garnish with the scallions, chilies, and cilantro leaves.

COOK'S TIP
The seafood packets will spread out when cooked so be sure to space them well apart in the steamer to prevent them sticking together.

ASPARAGUS WITH CREAMY RASPBERRY VINAIGRETTE

This simple starter is an unusual and delicious way to serve the first raspberries of the summer.

Serves 4

1½ pounds thin asparagus spears

2 tablespoons raspberry vinegar

½ teaspoon salt

1 teaspoon Dijon mustard

5 tablespoons sunflower oil

*2 tablespoons sour cream or
   plain yogurt*

white pepper

1 cup fresh raspberries

Fill a large pan, or wok with water about 4 inches deep and bring to a boil. Trim the ends of the asparagus spears. If desired, remove the "scales" using a vegetable peeler. Tie the asparagus into two bundles. Lower the bundles into the boiling water and cook for 2 minutes, until just tender.

With a slotted spatula, carefully remove the asparagus bundles from the boiling water and immerse in cold water to stop the cooking. Drain and untie the bundles. Pat dry. Chill the asparagus at least 1 hour.

Put the vinegar and salt in a bowl and stir to dissolve. Add the mustard, then gradually stir in the oil until blended. Add the sour cream or yogurt and pepper to taste.

To serve, place the asparagus on individual plates and drizzle the dressing across the middle of the spears. Garnish with the fresh raspberries.

savory dishes

By partnering fruit with vegetables, fish, shellfish,

poultry, game or meat, stunningly successful savory

dishes, many of them with an international flavor, can be

created. Here you will find plenty of inspiration for

mouthwatering main courses and extra-special recipes

perfect for entertaining.

LEMON AND GINGER SPICY BEANS

An extremely quick delicious meal, made with canned beans for speed.

Serves 4

2 tablespoons chopped fresh ginger root

3 garlic cloves, roughly chopped

1 cup cold water

1 tablespoon sunflower oil

1 large onion, thinly sliced

1 fresh red chili, seeded and
  finely chopped

1/4 teaspoon cayenne pepper

2 teaspoons ground cumin

1 teaspoon ground coriander

1/2 teaspoon ground turmeric

2 tablespoons lemon juice

1/2 cup chopped fresh cilantro

14-ounce can black-eyed peas, drained
  and rinsed

14-ounce can aduki beans, drained
  and rinsed

14-ounce can navy beans, drained
  and rinsed

salt and ground black pepper

Place the ginger, garlic and 4 tablespoons of the cold water in a blender or food processor and blend until smooth. Set aside.

Heat the oil in a pan. Add the onion and chili and cook gently for 5 minutes until the vegetables are softened.

Add the cayenne pepper, cumin, ground coriander and turmeric and stir-fry for 1 minute.

Stir in the ginger and garlic paste from the blender and cook for another minute, stirring to prevent sticking.

Add the remaining water, lemon juice and fresh cilantro, stir well and bring to a boil. Cover the pan tightly and cook for 5 minutes.

Add all the beans and cook for a further 5–10 minutes. Season with salt and pepper to taste and serve.

APPLE, ONION, AND GRUYÈRE TART

Serve this tart with baked potatoes for a more filling meal.

Serves 4–6

1 large onion, finely chopped
2 tablespoons butter
1 large or 2 small eating apples,
*   peeled and grated*
2 eggs
²⁄₃ cup heavy cream
¼ teaspoon dried mixed herbs
½ teaspoon dry mustard
4 ounces Gruyère cheese
salt and ground black pepper
green salad leaves, to serve

For the pastry
2 cups flour
¼ teaspoon dry mustard
6 tablespoons soft margarine
6 tablespoons Gruyère cheese,
*   finely grated*

COOK'S TIP
Instead of Gruyère, try Cheddar
or Emmenthaler cheese.

For the pastry, sift the flour, a pinch of salt, and the mustard into a bowl. Rub in the margarine and cheese, add 2 tablespoons water and form into a ball. Chill. Cook the onion in the butter for 10 minutes until softened. Stir in the apple and cook for 2–3 minutes. Let cool. Roll out the pastry and line a lightly greased 8-inch fluted quiche pan. Chill for 20 minutes. Preheat the oven to 400°F. Line the pastry with wax paper and fill with baking beans. Bake for 20 minutes. Beat together the eggs, cream, herbs, seasoning, and mustard. Grate three-quarters of the cheese and stir into this mixture. Slice the remaining cheese. When the pastry is cooked, remove the paper and beans, add the onion mixture and pour in the egg mixture. Arrange the sliced cheese on top. Turn the oven down to 375°F. Bake the tart for 20 minutes, until golden and just firm. Serve hot or warm with green salad leaves.

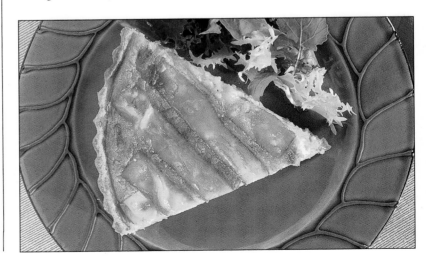

BANANA CURRY

The sweetness of the bananas combines well with the spices used to produce a mild, sweet curry.

Serves 4

4 under-ripe bananas

2 tbsp ground coriander

1 tbsp ground cumin

1 tsp chili powder

½ tsp salt

¼ tsp ground turmeric

1 tsp sugar

1 tbsp gram flour

3 tbsp chopped fresh cilantro

6 tbsp corn oil

¼ tsp cumin seeds

¼ tsp black mustard seeds

fresh sprigs of cilantro, to garnish

chappatis, to serve

COOK'S TIP
Choose bananas that are slightly under-ripe so that they retain their shape and do not become unpleasantly mushy when they are cooked.

Trim the bananas leaving the skin on, and cut each into three equal pieces. Make a lengthwise slit in each piece of banana, without cutting through.

Mix the coriander, cumin, chili powder, salt, turmeric, sugar, gram flour, and chopped cilantro in a soup plate. Stir in 1 tbsp of the oil. Carefully stuff each piece of banana with the spice mixture, taking care not to break them in half.

Heat the remaining oil in a large heavy-based saucepan and fry the cumin and mustard seeds for 2 minutes or until they begin to splutter. Add the bananas and toss gently in the oil. Cover and simmer over a low heat for 15 minutes, stirring from time to time, until the bananas are soft, but not mushy. Garnish with the fresh cilantro and serve with warm chappatis.

PLANTAIN AND VEGETABLE KEBABS

Tasty and colorful, these kebabs make a delightful main course for vegetarians or can be served as a side dish.

Serves 4

4oz pumpkin, peeled and cubed

1 red onion, cut into wedges

1 small zucchini, sliced

1 yellow plantain, sliced

1 eggplant, diced

½ red bell pepper, seeded and diced

½ green bell pepper, seeded and diced

12 button mushrooms, trimmed

4 tbsp lemon juice

4 tbsp olive or sunflower oil

3–4 tbsp soy sauce

⅔ cup tomato juice

*1 fresh green chili, seeded
    and chopped*

½ onion, grated

3 garlic cloves, crushed

*1½ tsp dried tarragon,
    crushed*

*¾ tsp each dried basil, dried thyme,
    and ground cinnamon*

2 tbsp butter

1¼ cups vegetable stock

freshly ground black pepper

Place the pumpkin in a small bowl and cover with boiling water. Blanch for 2–3 minutes, then drain, refresh under cold water, drain again, and tip into a large bowl. Add the red onion, zucchini, plantain, eggplant, bell peppers, and mushrooms.

Mix the lemon juice, oil, soy sauce, tomato juice, chili, grated onion, garlic, herbs, cinnamon, and black pepper in a pitcher. Pour over the vegetables. Toss well, then set aside in a cool place to marinate for 3–4 hours.

Drain the vegetables and thread them alternately onto eight skewers. Broil under a low heat for about 15 minutes, turning the kebabs frequently, until golden brown. Baste occasionally with the marinade to keep the vegetables moist.

Place the remaining marinade, butter, and stock in a pan and bring to a boil. Lower the heat and simmer for 10 minutes to cook the onion and reduce the sauce. Pour into a serving pitcher. Arrange the vegetable skewers on a plate. Serve with a rice dish or salad.

SEAFOOD KEBABS WITH GINGER AND LIME

This fragrant marinade will guarantee a mouthwatering aroma from the barbecue, and it is equally delicious with chicken or pork.

Serves 4–6

1¼ pounds shrimp and cubed monkfish
selection of prepared vegetables, such
*   as red, green or orange bell peppers,*
*   zucchini, button mushrooms, red*
*   onion and cherry tomatoes*
bay leaves

For the marinade
3 limes
1 tablespoon green cardamom pods
1 onion, finely chopped
1 tablespoon grated fresh ginger root
1 large garlic clove, skinned
*   and crushed*
3 tablespoons olive oil

First make the marinade. Finely grate the rind from one lime and squeeze the juice from all of them. Split the cardamom pods and remove the seeds. Crush the cardamom seeds in a pestle and mortar or with the back of a heavy-bladed knife.

Place the lime rind and juice, crushed cardamom, onion, ginger root, garlic and olive oil in a small bowl and mix together thoroughly. Pour the marinade over the shrimp and monkfish, stir gently, then cover and leave in a cool place for 2–3 hours.

Thread four skewers alternately with the shrimp, monkfish, vegetables and bay leaves. Cook slowly under a hot broiler or over a barbecue, basting occasionally with the marinade, until the shrimp, fish and vegetables are just cooked through and browned on the outside. Serve at once.

CLASSIC FISH PIE WITH LEMON

Instead of a potato topping, a crust of puff pastry could be used for a change.

Serves 4

*1 pound mixed raw fish such
    as cod or salmon fillets and
    peeled shrimp
finely grated rind of 1 lemon
1 pound potatoes
3 tablespoons butter
3 tablespoons all purpose flour
⅔ cup milk
3 tablespoons chopped fresh parsley
1 egg
salt and ground black pepper*

Preheat the oven to 425°F. Grease a 2-cup ovenproof dish. Cut the fish into bite-size pieces. Season the fish, sprinkle on the lemon rind and place in the base of the dish. Cook the potatoes in boiling, salted water until tender.

Meanwhile, make the sauce. Melt a third of the butter in a saucepan, add the flour and cook for a few minutes. Remove from the heat and gradually whisk in the milk. Return to the heat and bring to a boil. Simmer, whisking constantly, until the sauce has thickened. Add the parsley and season to taste. Pour over the fish.

Drain and mash the potatoes, adding the remaining butter. Pipe or spoon the potatoes on top of the fish mixture. Beat the egg and brush onto the potato. Bake for 45 minutes, until the top is golden.

BROILED SNAPPER WITH MANGO SALSA

A ripe mango is used in this fruity salsa with the tropical flavors of cilantro, ginger and chili.

Serves 4

12 ounces new potatoes

3 eggs

4 ounces green beans, trimmed
* and halved*

4 × 12-ounce red snapper, scaled
* and gutted*

2 tablespoons olive oil

6 ounces mixed lettuce leaves, such as
* frisée or oak leaf*

2 cherry tomatoes

salt and ground black pepper

For the salsa

3 tablespoons chopped fresh cilantro

1 medium-size ripe mango, peeled,
* pitted and diced*

1/2 red chili, seeded and chopped

1 tablespoon grated fresh ginger root

juice of 2 limes

generous pinch of celery salt

Bring the potatoes to a boil and simmer for 15–20 minutes. Drain. Bring another large saucepan of salted water to a boil. Put in the eggs and boil for 4 minutes, then add the beans and cook for a further 6 minutes. Remove the eggs from the pan, cool, peel and cut into quarters. Preheat the broiler. Slash the snappers on each side, moisten with oil and cook for 12 minutes, turning once. To make the salsa, place the cilantro in a blender or food processor. Add the remaining ingredients and process smoothly.

Arrange the lettuce leaves on four large plates. Arrange the snapper over the lettuce and season to taste. Halve the potatoes and tomatoes, and add with the beans and eggs to the salad. Serve with the salsa.

FISH WITH MANGO AND GINGER DRESSING

The tasty dressing for this salad combines the flavor of rich mango with ginger, hot chili, and lime.

Serves 4

1 large baguette (French bread)

4 redfish, black bream or porgy, each
weighing about 10 ounces

1 tablespoon vegetable oil

1 mango

1 tablespoon grated fresh ginger root

1 fresh red chili, seeded and
finely chopped

2 tablespoons lime juice

2 tablespoons chopped fresh cilantro

6 ounces young spinach

6 ounces cherry tomatoes, halved

COOK'S TIP
Other varieties of fish suitable
for use in this salad include
salmon, monkfish, tuna, sea
bass, and halibut.

Preheat the oven to 350°F. Cut the baguette into 8-inch lengths. Slice lengthwise, then cut into thick fingers. Place the bread on a cookie sheet and dry in the oven for 15 minutes. Preheat the broiler or light the barbecue. Slash the fish on both sides and moisten with oil. Broil or barbecue for about 6 minutes, turning once. Slice one half of the mango and reserve.

Place the remainder in a blender or food processor. Add the ginger, chili, lime juice, and cilantro. Process until smooth. Adjust to a pouring consistency with 2–3 tablespoons water.

Wash and dry the spinach, then arrange on four plates. Place the fish on top. Spoon on the dressing. Serve with mango slices, tomatoes and the bread.

BROILED FRESH SARDINES

Fresh sardines are flavorful and firm-fleshed, and quite different in taste and consistency from those canned in oil. They are excellent simply broiled and served with lemon.

Serves 4–6

2 pounds very fresh sardines, gutted and with heads removed

olive oil, for brushing

salt and ground black pepper

3 tablespoons chopped fresh parsley, to serve

lemon wedges, to garnish

Preheat the broiler. Rinse the sardines in water. Pat dry with paper towels. Brush the sardines lightly with olive oil and sprinkle generously with salt and ground black pepper. Place the sardines in one layer on the broiling pan. Broil the sardines for about 3–4 minutes.

Turn the sardines over, and cook for 3–4 minutes more, or until the skin just begins to brown. Serve immediately, sprinkled with parsley and garnished with lemon wedges.

WHITING FILLETS IN A LEMONY POLENTA CRUST

Polenta is the name given to fine golden cornmeal. Use the quick and easy polenta if you can as it will give a better crunchy coating for the fish.

Serves 4

8 small whiting fillets

finely grated rind of 2 lemons

2 cups polenta

2 tablespoons olive oil

1 tablespoon butter

salt and ground black pepper

steamed spinach, to serve

toasted pine nuts, ½ red onion, finely sliced, and 2 tablespoons mixed fresh herbs such as parsley, chervil and chives, to garnish

Make four small cuts in each whiting fillet, with a sharp knife to prevent the fish curling up when it is cooked.

Sprinkle the seasoning and half of the lemon rind over the fish.

Mix the polenta with the remaining lemon rind. Press the polenta on to the fillets. Chill for 30 minutes.

Heat the oil and butter in a large frying pan and gently fry the fillets on either side for 3–4 minutes. Serve with steamed spinach and garnish with toasted pine nuts, red onion slices, and the mixed fresh herbs.

SALMON WITH LEMON AND HERB BUTTER

Cooking "en papillote" preserves and enhances the flavor of salmon in this simple but delectable recipe.

Serves 4

4 tablespoons butter, softened

finely grated rind of ½ small lemon

1 tablespoon lemon juice

1 tablespoon chopped fresh dill

4 salmon steaks, about 5 ounces each

2 lemon slices, halved

4 fresh dill sprigs

salt and ground black pepper

Place the butter, lemon rind, lemon juice, chopped dill and seasoning in a small bowl and mix together with a fork until blended.

Spoon the butter on to a piece of waxed paper and roll up, smoothing with your hands into a sausage shape. Twist the ends tightly, wrap in plastic wrap and transfer to the freezer for 20 minutes, until firm.

Meanwhile, preheat the oven to 375°F. Cut out four squares of foil big enough to encase the salmon steaks and grease lightly. Place a salmon steak in the center of each one.

Remove the butter from the freezer and slice into eight rounds. Place two rounds on top of each salmon steak with a halved lemon slice in the center and a sprig of dill on top. Lift up the edges of the foil and crinkle them together until well sealed.

Lift the parcels on to a cookie sheet and bake for about 20 minutes.

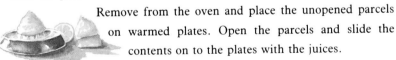

Remove from the oven and place the unopened parcels on warmed plates. Open the parcels and slide the contents on to the plates with the juices.

COOK'S TIP

A different selection of fresh herbs could be used to flavor the butter – try mint, fennel fronds, lemon balm, parsley or oregano instead of the dill.

SEA BASS WITH CITRUS FRUIT

Along the Mediterranean coast, sea bass is called loup de mer; *elsewhere in France it is known as* bar. *Its delicate flavor is complemented by citrus fruits and fruity French olive oil.*

Serves 6

1 lemon

1 orange

1 small grapefruit

1 sea bass (about 3 pounds), cleaned and scaled

6 fresh basil sprigs

6 fresh dill sprigs

flour, for dusting

3 tablespoons French olive oil

4–6 shallots, peeled and halved

4 tablespoons dry white wine

1 tablespoon butter

salt and ground black pepper

fresh dill, to garnish

With a vegetable peeler, remove the rind from the lemon, orange and grapefruit. Cut into thin julienne strips, cover and set aside. Peel off the white pith from the fruits and, working over a bowl to catch the juices, cut out the segments from the grapefruit and orange and set aside for the garnish. Slice the lemon thickly.

Preheat the oven to 375°F. Wipe the fish dry inside and out and season the cavity with salt and ground black pepper. Make three diagonal slashes on each side of the fish. Reserve a few basil and dill sprigs for the garnish and fill the cavity with the remaining basil and dill, the lemon slices and half the julienne strips of citrus rind.

Dust the fish lightly with flour. In a roasting pan or flameproof casserole large enough to hold the fish, heat 2 tablespoons of the olive oil over medium-high heat and cook the fish for about 1 minute until the skin just crisps and browns on one side. Add the shallots.

Place the fish in the oven and bake for about 15 minutes, then carefully turn the fish over and stir in the shallots. Drizzle the fish with the remaining oil and bake for 10–15 minutes more until the flesh is opaque throughout.

Carefully transfer the fish to a heated serving dish and remove and discard the cavity stuffing. Pour off any excess oil and add the wine and 2–3 tablespoons of the fruit juices to the pan. Bring to a boil over high heat, stirring. Stir in the remaining julienne strips of citrus rind and boil for 2–3 minutes, then whisk in the butter.

Spoon the shallots and sauce over the fish. Garnish with the reserved basil and dill, and the reserved grapefruit and orange segments.

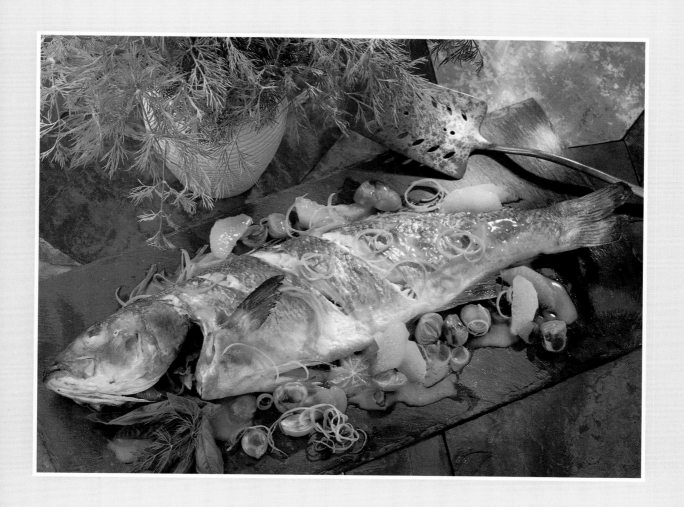

BAKED FISH IN BANANA LEAVES

Fish baked in banana leaves is particularly succulent and flavorful. This is a great dish for barbecuing.

Serves 4

1 cup coconut milk

2 tbsp red curry paste

3 tbsp fish sauce

2 tbsp superfine sugar

5 kaffir lime leaves, torn

4 fish fillets, about 6oz each

6oz mixed vegetables, such as carrots
   or leeks, finely shredded

4 banana leaves

For the garnish

2 tbsp shredded scallions

2 fresh red chilies, finely sliced

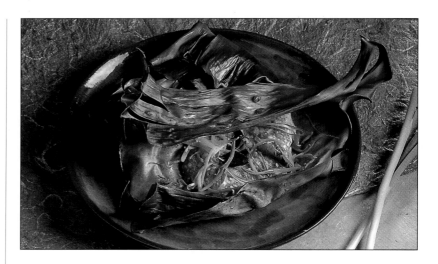

Combine the coconut milk, curry paste, fish sauce, sugar, and kaffir lime leaves in a shallow dish. Add the fish and marinate for 15–30 minutes. Preheat the oven to 400°F.

Mix the selected vegetables together and place a fourth of the mixture on top of a banana leaf. Place a fish fillet on top of each and moisten it with a little of its marinade.

Wrap the fish up by turning in the sides and ends of the leaf and securing the package with toothpicks. Repeat with the rest of the leaves, vegetables, and fish.

Bake for 20–25 minutes or until the fish is cooked. Alternatively, cook under the broiler or in a hinged broiler over a barbecue. Just before serving, garnish the fish with a sprinkling of scallions and sliced red chilies.

CHICKEN STEW WITH BLACKBERRIES AND LEMON BALM

The combination of red wine and blackberries in this delicious stew gives it a dramatic appearance.

Serves 4

4 chicken breasts, partly boned

2 tablespoons butter

1 tablespoon sunflower oil

4 tablespoons flour

²/₃ cup red wine

²/₃ cup chicken broth

grated rind of ¹/₂ orange plus
* 1 tablespoon juice*

3 lemon balm sprigs, finely chopped,
* plus a few extra sprigs to garnish*

²/₃ cup heavy cream

1 egg yolk

salt and ground black pepper

²/₃ cup fresh blackberries, plus ¹/₃ cup
* to garnish*

Remove any skin from the chicken, and season the meat. Heat the butter and oil in a pan, fry the chicken to seal it, then transfer to a casserole. Stir the flour into the pan, add the wine and broth and bring to a boil. Add the orange rind and juice, and the lemon balm. Pour over the chicken.

Preheat the oven to 350°F. Cover the casserole and cook in the oven for about 40 minutes.

Blend the cream with the egg yolk, add some of the liquid from the casserole and stir back into the dish with the blackberries. Cover and cook for a further 10–15 minutes. Serve garnished with the rest of the blackberries and lemon balm sprigs.

TAGINE OF CHICKEN

Lemon slices add a decorative and tangy touch to this richly spiced North African dish.

Serves 8

8 chicken legs (thighs and drumsticks)

2 tablespoons olive oil

1 medium onion, finely chopped

2 garlic cloves, crushed

1 teaspoon ground turmeric

½ teaspoon ground ginger

½ teaspoon ground cinnamon

scant 2 cups fresh or canned
  chicken broth

1¼ cups green olives, pitted

1 lemon, sliced

2½ cups fresh or canned chicken broth

1 pound couscous

4 zucchini, thickly sliced

2 carrots, thickly sliced

2 small turnips, peeled and cubed

3 tablespoons olive oil

15-ounce can chick-peas, drained

1 tablespoon chopped fresh cilantro

salt and ground black pepper

fresh cilantro sprigs, to garnish

Preheat the oven to 350°F. Cut the chicken legs into two through the joint. Heat the oil in a large flameproof casserole and, working in batches, brown the chicken on both sides. Remove the chicken and keep warm.

Add the onion and crushed garlic to the flameproof casserole and cook gently until tender. Add the spices and cook for 1 minute. Pour over the broth, bring to a boil, and return the chicken to the casserole. Cover and bake for 45 minutes until tender.

Transfer the chicken to a bowl, cover and keep warm. Remove any fat from the cooking liquid and boil to reduce by one third. Meanwhile, blanch the olives and lemon slices in a pan of boiling water for 2 minutes until the lemon skin is tender. Drain and add to the chicken with the reduced cooking liquid, adjusting the seasoning to taste.

To cook the couscous, bring the broth to the boil in a large pan and sprinkle in the couscous slowly, stirring all the time. Remove from the heat, cover and leave to stand for 5 minutes.

Meanwhile, cook the vegetables, drain and put them into a large bowl. Add the couscous and oil and season. Stir the grains to fluff them up, add the chick-peas and finally the chopped cilantro. Spoon on to a large serving plate, cover with the chicken pieces, and spoon over the liquid. Garnish with fresh cilantro sprigs.

HONEY AND ORANGE-GLAZED CHICKEN

Try orange-blossom honey for this tasty glaze. It makes a perfect partner for chicken and oranges.

Serves 4

4 chicken breasts, 6 ounces each,
  boned and skinned
1 tablespoon oil
4 scallions, chopped
1 garlic clove, crushed
3 tablespoons clear honey
¼ cup fresh orange juice
1 orange, peeled and segmented
2 tablespoons soy sauce
fresh lemon balm or flat-leaf parsley
  sprigs, to garnish
baked potatoes and salad, to serve

VARIATION
*The sauce is equally good when
served with pork chops.*

Preheat the oven to 375°F. Place the chicken breasts in a shallow roasting pan and set aside.

Heat the oil in a small pan. Fry the scallions and crushed garlic for 2 minutes, until softened. Add the honey, orange juice, orange segments and soy sauce to the pan, stirring well until the honey has dissolved.

Pour the mixture over the chicken and bake, uncovered, for 45 minutes, basting once or twice, until the chicken is cooked through. Serve on plates, garnished with lemon balm or parsley, accompanied by baked potatoes and a fresh salad.

LEMON CHICKEN STIR-FRY

It is essential to prepare all the ingredients before you begin as this dish is cooked in minutes.

Serves 4

4 chicken breasts, (about 5 ounces
  each), boned and skinned

1 tablespoon light soy sauce

5 tablespoons cornstarch

1 garlic clove, crushed

1 tablespoon superfine sugar

2 tablespoons dry sherry

²/₃ cup fresh or canned chicken broth

juice and finely shredded rind of 1
  lemon

4 tablespoons olive oil

1 bunch scallions, sliced diagonally into
  ¹/₂-inch pieces

salt and ground black pepper

Divide each chicken breast into two natural fillets. Place them between two sheets of plastic wrap and flatten to a thickness of ¼ inch with a rolling pin. Cut into 1-inch strips across the fillets. Put the chicken into a bowl with the soy sauce, then toss in 4 tablespoons of the cornstarch.

Have ready the garlic clove, sugar, sherry, broth, lemon juice, lemon rind, and the remaining cornstarch blended to a paste with cold water.

Heat the oil in a wok or large frying pan and cook the chicken in batches for 3–4 minutes. Remove and keep warm while frying the rest of the chicken.

Add the scallions and garlic to the pan and cook for about 2 minutes. Add the remaining ingredients with the chicken and bring to a boil, stirring until thickened and the chicken is evenly covered with the sauce. Serve immediately.

TURKEY WITH LEMON AND SAGE

Lemon and sage combine to give a lively Mediterranean flavor to this dish.

Serves 4

4 turkey cutlets (boneless slices of
*   breast), about 6 ounces each*
1 tablespoon freshly grated lemon rind
1 tablespoon chopped fresh sage, or
*   1 teaspoon dried sage*
¼ cup fresh lemon juice
6 tablespoons vegetable oil
1 cup fine dry bread crumbs
salt and ground black pepper
fresh sage leaves and lemon slices,
*   to garnish*

Place each cutlet between two sheets of wax paper. With the flat side of a meat pounder, pound the cutlets until about ¼-inch thick, being careful not to split the meat. Remove the wax paper. Sprinkle the cutlets with salt and pepper.

In a small bowl, combine the lemon rind, chopped sage, lemon juice and 2 tablespoons of the oil. Stir well to mix.

Arrange the turkey cutlets, in one layer, in one or two shallow baking dishes. Divide the lemon mixture evenly between the dishes and rub well into the turkey. Let marinate for 20 minutes.

Heat the remaining oil in a frying pan. Dredge the turkey scaloppine in the bread crumbs, shaking off the excess. Fry until golden brown, about 2 minutes on each side. Serve, garnished with sage leaves and lemon slices.

VARIATION
For a delicious alternative,
substitute fresh tarragon leaves
for the sage.

GUINEA HEN WITH CIDER AND APPLES

Guinea hens are farmed, so they are available quite frequently in supermarkets, usually fresh. Their flavor is reminiscent of an old-fashioned chicken – not really gamey, but they do have slightly darker meat.

Serves 4

4–4¹/₂-pound guinea hen

1 onion, halved

3 celery stalks

3 bay leaves

a little butter

1¹/₄ cups hard cider

²/₃ cup chicken broth

*2 small firm, tart cooking apples (about
    1 pound), peeled and sliced*

4 tablespoons thick heavy cream

a few sage leaves, plus extra to garnish

2 tablespoons chopped fresh parsley

salt and ground black pepper

If the guinea hen is packed with its giblets, put them in a pan with water to cover, add half the onion, a stalk of celery, a bay leaf and seasoning. Bring to a boil and simmer for about 30 minutes, or until you have about ²/₃ cup well-flavored stock. Use this in the recipe instead of the chicken broth.

Preheat the oven to 375°F. Wash and wipe dry the bird and place the remaining onion half and a tablespoon of butter inside the body cavity. Place the guinea hen in a roasting dish, sprinkle with seasoning, and dot with a few pieces of butter.

Pour the cider and chicken broth or homemade stock into the dish and cover with a lid or foil. Bake in the oven for 25 minutes per pound, basting the bird occasionally.

Uncover for the last 20 minutes and baste well again. Slice the remaining celery and add it together with the prepared apples. When the guinea hen is cooked, transfer it to a warm serving dish and keep warm. Remove the apples and celery with a slotted spoon and set aside.

Boil the liquid rapidly to reduce to about ²/₃ cup. Stir in the cream, seasoning, and the sage leaves, and cook for a few minutes more to reduce slightly. Return the apples to this pan with the parsley and warm through. Serve with or around the bird, garnished with sage leaves.

NORMANDY PHEASANT

Cider, apples, and cream make this a rich, flavorful dish – a great change from a plain roast.

Serves 4

2 oven-ready pheasants

1 tablespoon olive oil

2 tablespoons butter

4 tablespoons Calvados or Apple Jack

1⅞ cups hard cider

bouquet garni

*3 crisp eating apples, peeled, cored
and thickly sliced*

⅔ cup heavy cream

salt and ground black pepper

thyme sprigs, to garnish

Preheat the oven to 325°F. Joint both pheasants into four pieces using a large sharp knife. Discard the backbones and knuckles.

Heat the oil and butter in a large flameproof casserole. Working in two batches, add the pheasant pieces to the casserole and brown them over high heat. Return all the pheasant pieces to the casserole.

Standing well back, pour over the Calvados or Apple Jack and set it alight. When the flames have subsided, pour in the cider, then add the bouquet garni and seasoning and bring to a boil. Cover the casserole and cook in the oven for 50 minutes.

Tuck the apple slices around the pheasant. Cover and cook for about 5–10 minutes, or until the pheasant is tender. Transfer the pheasant and apple to a warmed serving plate. Keep warm.

Remove the bouquet garni, then boil the liquid to reduce the sauce by half until you have a syrupy consistency. Stir in the cream and simmer for 2–3 minutes more until thickened. Taste the sauce and adjust the seasoning if necessary. Spoon the sauce over the pheasant and serve immediately garnished with thyme sprigs.

STIR-FRIED DUCK WITH BLUEBERRIES

Serve this conveniently quick dinner party dish with fresh mint sprigs, which will give a wonderful fresh aroma as you bring the meal to the table.

Serves 4

2 duck breasts, about 6 ounces each

2 tablespoons sunflower oil

1 tablespoon red wine vinegar

1 teaspoon sugar

1 teaspoon red wine

1 teaspoon crème de cassis (black currant liqueur)

1 cup fresh blueberries

1 tablespoon chopped fresh mint

salt and ground black pepper

fresh mint sprigs, to garnish

Cut the duck breasts crosswise into thin slices. Season the slices of duck well with salt and pepper.

Heat a wok or large frying pan and add the sunflower oil. When the oil is hot, add the slices of duck and stir-fry for 3 minutes.

Add the red wine vinegar, sugar, red wine and crème de cassis. Bubble for 3 minutes, to reduce the sauce to a thick syrup.

Stir in the blueberries, sprinkle over the mint and serve immediately garnished with fresh mint sprigs.

LAMB, LEEK, AND APPLE PIE

An innovative combination where lamb and leeks are spiced up with apple.

Serves 4

*1½ pounds lamb neck fillets, cut into
   12 pieces*

4 ounces bacon, diced

1 onion, thinly sliced

12 ounces leeks, sliced

*1 large firm, tart cooking apple (about
   8 ounces), peeled, cored and sliced*

¼–½ teaspoon ground allspice

¼–½ teaspoon grated nutmeg

⅔ cup lamb, beef or vegetable broth

8 ounces ready-made pie pastry

beaten egg or milk, to glaze

salt and ground black pepper

COOK'S TIP

*When you are buying leeks, look
for those that are straight and
well shaped. Avoid any that
have yellow, discolored and
slimy leaves.*

Preheat the oven to 400°F. Layer the meats, onion, leeks, and apple in a 3¾-cup pie dish, sprinkling in the spices and seasoning as you go. Pour in the broth.

On a lightly floured surface, roll out the pastry to ¾ inch larger than the top of the pie dish. Cut a narrow strip from around the pastry, fit it around the dampened rim of the dish, then brush with water.

Lay the pastry over the filling, and press the edges together to seal them. Brush the top with beaten egg or milk, and make a hole in the center.

Bake the pie for 20 minutes, then reduce the oven temperature to 350°F and continue to bake for 1–1¼ hours, covering the pie with foil if the pastry begins to become too brown. Serve immediately.

VENISON WITH CRANBERRY SAUCE

Venison steaks are now readily available. Lean and low in fat, they are the healthy choice for a special occasion. Served with a sauce of fresh seasonal cranberries, port and ginger, they make a dish with a wonderful combination of flavors.

Serves 4

1 orange

1 lemon

*¾ cup fresh or frozen cranberries,
    picked over*

1 teaspoon grated fresh ginger root

1 thyme sprig

1 teaspoon Dijon mustard

4 tablespoons red currant jelly

⅔ cup ruby port

2 tablespoons sunflower oil

4 venison steaks

2 shallots, finely chopped

salt and ground black pepper

thyme sprigs, to garnish

*creamy mashed potatoes and broccoli,
    to serve*

Pare the rind from half the orange and half the lemon using a vegetable peeler, then cut into very fine strips.

Blanch the strips in a small pan of boiling water for about 5 minutes until tender. Drain the strips and refresh under cold water.

Squeeze the juice from the orange and lemon and then pour into a small pan. Add the fresh or frozen cranberries, ginger, thyme sprig, mustard, red currant jelly and port. Cook over low heat until the jelly melts.

Bring the sauce to a boil, stirring occasionally, then cover the pan and reduce the heat. Cook gently, for about 15 minutes, until the cranberries are just tender.

Heat the oil in a heavy-based frying pan, add the venison steaks and cook over high heat for 2–3 minutes.

Turn over the steaks and add the shallots to the pan. Cook the steaks on the other side for 2–3 minutes, depending on whether you like rare or medium-cooked meat.

Just before the end of cooking, pour in the sauce and add the strips of orange and lemon rind.

Leave the sauce to bubble for a few seconds to thicken slightly, then remove the thyme sprig and adjust the seasoning to taste.

Transfer the venison steaks to warmed serving plates and spoon the sauce over the meat. Garnish each plate with thyme sprigs and serve accompanied by creamy mashed potatoes and broccoli.

BEEF STRIPS WITH ORANGE AND GINGER

Tender strips of beef, tangy ginger and crisp carrot make a simple but delicious stir-fry.

Serves 4

1 pound lean beef rump, fillet,
*   or sirloin*
finely grated rind and juice of 1 orange
1 tablespoon light soy sauce
1 teaspoon cornstarch
1 tablespoon chopped ginger root
2 teaspoons sesame oil
1 large carrot, cut into thin strips
2 scallions, thinly sliced

Cut the beef into thin strips crosswise using a large sharp knife. Place the beef strips in a bowl and sprinkle over the orange rind and juice. Leave to marinate in a cool place for at least 30 minutes, or overnight in the fridge.

When ready to cook, drain the liquid from the meat and set aside, then mix the meat with the soy sauce, cornstarch and ginger.

Heat the oil in a wok or large frying pan over a medium-high heat and add the beef. Stir-fry for 1 minute until the meat is lightly colored, then add the carrot and stir-fry for 2–3 minutes more.

Stir in the scallions and the reserved marinating liquid, then cook, stirring constantly, until boiling and thickened. Serve the stir-fry hot with rice noodles or plain boiled rice.

COOK'S TIP

Large wok lids are cumbersome
and can be difficult to store in a
small kitchen. Instead of using a
lid, place a circle of wax paper
over the food surface to retain
the cooking juices.

PORK AND APPLE HOT-POT

An economical and tasty dish using a cheaper cut of pork.

Serves 4

1¼ pounds sparerib pork chops

2 tablespoons sunflower oil

1 large onion, sliced

3 celery stalks, chopped

1 tablespoon chopped fresh sage, or
    1 teaspoon dried

1 tablespoon chopped fresh parsley

2 eating apples, peeled, cored and cut
    into thick wedges

⅔ cup apple juice

⅔ cup broth

1 tablespoon cornstarch

1 pound par-boiled, peeled and
    sliced potatoes

melted butter, to glaze

salt and ground black pepper

sage leaves, to garnish

Remove any bones from the pork and cut the meat into even-size cubes. Sprinkle with seasoning.

Heat the oil in a pan and fry the onion and celery until golden. Remove and place half in the base of a casserole. Arrange the meat on top and sprinkle with half the herbs.

Add the apples and the rest of the onion, celery, and herbs. Season to taste. Blend the apple juice with the broth and cornstarch and pour over.

Preheat the oven to 375°F. Top with the sliced potatoes and brush with melted butter. Cover and cook in the oven for 50–60 minutes, removing the lid for the last 15 minutes to brown the potatoes. Serve immediately, garnished with sage leaves.

SOMERSET PORK WITH APPLES

A rich, country dish using fresh apples and cider.

Serves 4

2 tablespoons butter

*1¼ pounds pork loin, cut into
   bite-size pieces*

12 baby onions, peeled

2 teaspoons grated lemon rind

1¼ cups hard cider

⅔ cup veal broth

2 eating apples, cored and sliced

3 tablespoons chopped fresh parsley

scant ½ cup whipping cream

salt and ground black pepper

COOK'S TIP

*It is advisable to remove the rind
from the pork before cutting into
pieces. This is best done with
sharp scissors or a sharp knife.*

Heat the butter in a large heavy-based frying pan and sauté the pork in batches until brown. Transfer the pork to a bowl.

Add the onions to the pan, brown lightly, then stir in the lemon rind, cider, and broth and boil for about 3 minutes. Return all the pork to the pan and cook gently for about 25 minutes until the pork is tender.

Stir the apples into the pan and cook for 5 minutes more. Using a slotted spoon, transfer the pork, onions, and apples to a warmed serving dish, cover and keep warm. Add the parsley and stir the cream into the pan and allow to bubble to thicken the sauce slightly. Season, then pour over the pork and serve immediately.

cold desserts

Fabulous fruit, nutritious, colorful and brimming with flavor, makes the best cold desserts. Enjoy a wide range of dishes, from simple creations such as Pears with Honey and Wine, where one fruit stands alone in all its glory to international favorites such as Summer Fruit Dessert, to heavenly treats such as Raspberry and Nectarine Pavlova, and favorite combinations with a new twist such as Frozen Apple and Blackberry Terrine.

TROPICAL BANANA FRUIT SALAD

Not surprisingly, bananas go particularly well with other tropical fruits.

Serves 4–6

1 medium pineapple

14oz can guava halves
  in syrup

1 large mango, peeled, pitted,
  and diced

2 medium bananas

²⁄₃ cup preserved ginger, plus 2 tbsp
  of the syrup

4 tbsp thick coconut milk

2 tsp sugar

½ tsp freshly grated nutmeg

½ tsp ground cinnamon

strips of fresh coconut, to decorate

COOK'S TIP

For an appealing decorative touch, use two small pineapples. Cut them in half, through the leaves, carefully scoop out the pulp, and use the shells as containers for the tropical fruit salad.

Peel the pineapple, remove the core, cut the flesh into cubes, and place in a large serving bowl. Drain the guavas, reserving the syrup, and chop them into dice. Add the guavas and mango to the bowl. Slice one of the bananas, and add it to the bowl.

Chop the preserved ginger and add it to the pineapple mixture. Mix together lightly. Pour the ginger syrup into a blender or food processor. Add the reserved guava syrup, coconut milk, and sugar. Slice the remaining banana and add to the mixture. Blend to a smooth, creamy purée.

Pour the banana and coconut purée mixture over the fruit, adding the freshly grated nutmeg and ground cinnamon. Serve the fruit salad chilled, decorated with strips of coconut.

Watermelon, Ginger and Grapefruit Salad

This combination of fruit and ginger is very light and refreshing for a summer meal.

Serves 4

2 cups diced watermelon flesh

2 ruby or pink grapefruit

2 pieces preserved ginger in syrup

2 tablespoons preserved ginger syrup

Cook's tip

Toss the fruits gently – grapefruit segments will break up easily and the appearance of the dish will be spoiled.

Remove any seeds from the watermelon and cut the flesh into bite-size chunks. Using a small sharp knife, cut away all the peel and pith from the grapefruits and carefully lift out the segments, catching any juice.

Finely chop the preserved ginger and place in a serving bowl with the melon cubes and grapefruit segments, adding the reserved juice. Spoon the ginger syrup over the fruits and toss lightly together.

GINGER AND HONEY WINTER FRUITS

A compote of dried fruit flavored with honey is equally tasty as a dessert or breakfast dish. Serve it with yogurt or cream.

Serves 4

1 lemon

4 green cardamom pods

1 cinnamon stick

⅔ cup clear honey

2 tablespoons ginger syrup, from the jar

2½ cups assorted dried fruits

1-inch piece fresh ginger

1 orange, peeled and segmented

VARIATION
Omit the ginger syrup and use 2 tablespoons rosewater instead. Add ½ cup blanched almonds as well.

Thinly pare 2 strips of rind from the lemon. Lightly crush the cardamom pods with the back of a heavy-bladed knife. Place the lemon rind, cardamoms, cinnamon stick, honey and ginger syrup in a heavy saucepan. Pour in ¼ cup water and add the dried fruit. Bring to a boil, then lower the heat and simmer for 10 minutes. Pour into a serving bowl. Set aside until cool.

Chop the ginger finely and stir it into the fruit salad, with the orange segments. Cover and chill until ready to serve.

BLUEBERRY AND ORANGE SALAD WITH LAVENDER MERINGUES

Delicate blueberries and tangy oranges are combined with tiny lavender-flavored meringues in this simple, but stunning salad. Lavender sprigs add the final decorative touch.

Serves 4

6 oranges

3 cups blueberries

8 fresh lavender sprigs

For the meringue

2 egg whites

½ cup superfine sugar

1 teaspoon fresh lavender flowers

> **COOK'S TIP**
> *Lavender is used in both sweet and savory dishes. Always use fresh or recently dried flowers, and avoid artificially scented bunches that are sold for domestic purposes. Of course, if you can't find fresh lavender, then you could just make plain meringues instead.*

Preheat the oven to 275°F. Line a cookie sheet with six layers of newspaper and cover with buttered waxed paper. Whisk the egg whites in a large mixing bowl until they hold soft peaks. Add the sugar a little at a time, whisking thoroughly after each addition. Fold in the lavender flowers.

Spoon the meringue into a pastry bag fitted with a ¼-inch plain nozzle. Pipe as many small buttons of meringue on to the prepared cookie sheet as you can. Bake the meringue near the bottom of the oven for 1½–2 hours.

To segment the oranges, remove the peel from the top, bottom, and sides with a serrated knife. Loosen the segments by cutting with a paring knife between the flesh and the membranes, holding the fruit over a bowl.

Arrange the segments on four plates. Combine the blueberries with the meringues and pile in the center of each plate. Decorate with sprigs of lavender and serve.

STRAWBERRIES WITH COINTREAU

Strawberries are one of summer's greatest pleasures. Try this simple way to serve them.

Serves 4

1 orange

3 tablespoons sugar

5 tablespoons water

3 tablespoons Cointreau or
  orange liqueur

3 cups strawberries, hulled

1 cup whipping cream

VARIATION

Instead of using strawberries on their own in this dessert, add a mixture of other fresh seasonal berries, such as raspberries and blueberries, along with sliced summer fruits like peaches and nectarines.

Peel wide strips of rind without the pith from the orange and cut into very thin julienne strips. Combine the sugar and water in a small saucepan. Bring to a boil over high heat, swirling the pan occasionally to dissolve the sugar. Add the julienne strips and simmer for 10 minutes. Remove the pan from the heat and let the syrup cool completely, then stir in the Cointreau. Reserve four strawberries for decoration and cut the rest lengthwise in halves or quarters. Put them in a bowl and add the syrup and orange rind. Set aside for 2 hours. Whip the cream and sweeten to taste. Serve the strawberries with cream and the reserved strawberries.

ICED PINEAPPLE CRUSH WITH STRAWBERRIES AND LYCHEES

The sweet tropical flavors of pineapple and lychees mixed with strawberries make this a refreshing salad.

Serves 4

2 small pineapples

3 cups strawberries

14-ounce can lychees

3 tablespoons Kirsch or white rum

2 tablespoons confectioner's sugar

COOK'S TIP

A ripe pineapple will resist pressure when squeezed and will have a sweet, fragrant smell. In winter, freezing conditions can cause the flesh to blacken.

Remove the crown from both pineapples by twisting sharply. Reserve the leaves for decoration. Cut the fruit in half diagonally with a large serrated knife. Cut around the flesh inside the skin with a small serrated knife, keeping the skin intact. Remove the core from the pineapple.

Chop the pineapple and combine with the strawberries and lychees. Combine the Kirsch or white rum with the confectioner's sugar, pour over the fruit, and freeze for 45 minutes. Spoon the semi-frozen fruit into the pineapple skins and decorate with pineapple leaves.

MIXED FRUIT AND BERRY SALAD WITH COFFEE CREAM

The inspiration for this refreshing sweet salad came from Japan. Scented fruits and berries are mixed together and served with minted coffee cream, which is excellent with fresh fruit.

Serves 6

1 small fresh pineapple

2 large ripe pears

2 fresh peaches

12 strawberries

12 canned lychees and the juice from the can

6 small mint sprigs, plus extra sprigs to decorate

1 tablespoon instant coffee granules

2 tablespoons boiling water

2/3 cup heavy cream

VARIATION

Use fresh lychees when they are in season. Choose fruit with a pink or red skin which indicates that the lychee will be sweet and ripe. The skin is brittle and peels off easily and the fruit should be pearly white.

Peel and pit the fruit as necessary and chop into even-size pieces. Place all the fruit in a large glass bowl and pour on the lychee juice. Chill until ready to serve.

To make the sauce, remove the leaves from the mint sprigs and place them in a food processor or blender with the instant coffee granules and boiling water. Blend until smooth. Add the cream and process again briefly.

Serve the fruit salad decorated with small mint sprigs, and hand the coffee sauce separately.

BANANA AND MELON IN ORANGE VANILLA SAUCE

A chilled banana and melon compote in a delicious orange sauce makes a perfect summer dessert.

Serves 4

1¼ cups orange juice

1 vanilla bean

1 tsp finely grated orange rind

1 tbsp sugar

4 ripe, but firm, bananas

1 honeydew melon

2 tbsp lemon juice

strips of blanched orange rind, to
*   decorate (optional)*

COOK'S TIP

Most large supermarkets and
health food stores sell vanilla
beans. If they are unavailable,
use a few drops of vanilla
extract instead. Wash, dry, and
store the bean to use again.

Place the orange juice in a small saucepan with the vanilla bean, orange rind, and sugar. Heat gently, stirring until the sugar has dissolved, then bring to a boil.

Lower the heat and simmer gently for 15 minutes or until the sauce is syrupy. Remove from the heat and leave to cool. Remove the vanilla bean. If using vanilla extract, stir into the sauce once it has cooled.

Roughly chop the bananas and melon, place in a large serving bowl, and toss with the lemon juice. Pour the cooled sauce over and chill the compote. Decorate with the blanched orange rind, if using, before serving.

RASPBERRY SALAD WITH MANGO CUSTARD SAUCE

This attractive salad combines sharp-flavored fresh raspberries and fragrant mango with two special sauces made from the same fruits.

Serves 4

1 large mango

3 egg yolks

2 tablespoons superfine sugar

2 teaspoons cornstarch

scant 1 cup milk

8 fresh mint sprigs, to decorate

For the raspberry sauce

3¹/₃ cups raspberries

3 tablespoons superfine sugar

COOK'S TIP

Mangoes are ripe when they yield to gentle pressure in the hand. Some varieties show a red-gold or yellow flush when they are ready to eat.

To prepare the mango, remove the top and bottom with a serrated knife. Cut away the outer skin, then remove the flesh by cutting either side of the flat central pit. Save one half of the fruit for decoration and roughly chop the remainder of the flesh.

To make the custard sauce, combine the egg yolks, sugar, cornstarch and 2 tablespoons of the milk smoothly in a bowl.

Rinse a small saucepan out with cold water to prevent the milk from catching. Bring the rest of the milk to a boil in the pan, pour it over the ingredients in the bowl, and stir evenly.

Strain the mixture back into the saucepan. Cook over low heat, stirring constantly, until the mixture thickens enough to coat the back of a spoon.

Pour the custard sauce into a food processor or blender, add the chopped mango, and blend until smooth. Let cool.

To make the raspberry sauce, place 2 cups of the raspberries in a stainless-steel saucepan. Add the sugar, soften over a gentle heat, and simmer for 5 minutes. Using a wooden spoon, force the fruit through a fine nylon strainer to remove the seeds. Let cool.

Spoon the raspberry sauce and mango custard sauce into 2 pools on 4 plates. Slice the reserved mango and fan out or arrange in a pattern over the raspberry sauce. Scatter fresh raspberries over the mango custard sauce. Decorate each with mint sprigs and serve.

SUMMER BERRY SALAD WITH FRESH MANGO SAUCE

When you only have a few berries, combine them with other summer fruits to make a colorful and refreshing fruit salad. Serve it simply with cream or ice cream, or drizzle with a vibrant mango sauce.

Serves 6

1 large ripe mango, peeled, pitted
   and chopped
rind of 1 orange
juice of 3 oranges
superfine sugar, to taste
2 peaches
2 nectarines
1 small mango, peeled
2 plums
1 pear or ½ small melon
juice of 1 lemon
2 heaping tablespoons wild
   strawberries (optional)
2 heaping tablespoons raspberries
2 heaping tablespoons blueberries
small mint sprigs, to decorate

Process the large mango in a food processor until smooth. Add the orange rind, juice and sugar to taste and process again until very smooth. Press through a strainer into a bowl and chill the sauce.

Peel the peaches, if desired, then slice and pit the peaches, nectarines, small mango and plums. Quarter the pear and remove the core and seeds, or, if using, slice the melon thinly and remove the peel.

Place the sliced fruits on a large plate, sprinkle the fruits with the lemon juice and chill, covered with plastic wrap, for up to 3 hours before serving. (Some fruits may discolor if cut too far ahead).

To serve, arrange the sliced fruits on serving plates, spoon the berries on top, drizzle with a little mango sauce and decorate with mint sprigs. Serve the remaining sauce separately.

STRAWBERRIES WITH RASPBERRY AND PASSIONFRUIT SAUCE

Strawberries release their finest flavor when served with raspberry and passionfruit sauce.

Serves 4

2 cups raspberries, fresh or frozen

3 tablespoons superfine sugar

2 passionfruits

4 cups small strawberries

8 plain butter cookies, to serve

Place the raspberries and sugar in a saucepan and soften over a gentle heat stirring occasionally, until simmering. Cook gently for 5 minutes, then let cool. Halve the passionfruits and scoop out the seeds and juice. Transfer the raspberries to a food processor or blender, add the passionfruit pulp, and blend for a few seconds.

Press the sauce through a fine nylon strainer to remove the seeds. Fold the strawberries into the sauce, then spoon into four stemmed glasses. Serve with plain butter cookies.

COOK'S TIP

When buying strawberries, choose fruit that is brightly colored, firm and unblemished. For the best flavor, serve the berries at room temperature. The delicate flavor will then be at its most intense.

FIG AND PEAR COMPOTE WITH RASPBERRIES

A simple yet sophisticated dessert featuring succulent, ripe autumnal fruits, enhanced by tangy raspberries.

Serves 4

6 tablespoons superfine sugar

1 bottle red wine

1 vanilla bean, split

1 strip pared lemon rind

4 pears

2 purple figs, quartered

1 1/3 cups fresh raspberries

lemon juice, to taste

Put the sugar and wine in a large pan and heat gently until dissolved. Add the vanilla bean and lemon rind and bring to a boil. Simmer for 5 minutes. Peel and halve the pears, then scoop out the cores, using a melon baller. Add the pears to the syrup and poach for 15 minutes, turning the pears several times so they color evenly. Add the figs and poach for 5 minutes.

Transfer the pears and figs to a serving bowl using a slotted spoon, then scatter over the raspberries. Return the syrup to the heat and boil rapidly to reduce slightly. Add a little lemon juice to taste. Strain the syrup over the fruits and serve warm.

PEARS WITH HONEY AND WINE

California produces several types of honey, the best known being sage blossom and alfalfa. In this Californian recipe, honey sweetens a mulled wine mixture used for stewing pears.

Serves 4

1 bottle of red Zinfandel wine

¾ cup granulated sugar

3 tablespoons clear honey

juice of ½ lemon

1 cinnamon stick

1 vanilla pod, split open lengthwise,
*   or a few drops of vanilla extract*

2-inch piece pared orange rind

1 whole clove

1 black peppercorn

4 firm ripe pears

whipped cream or sour cream,
*   to serve*

In a saucepan just large enough to hold the pears standing upright, combine the wine, sugar, honey, lemon juice, cinnamon stick, vanilla pod, orange rind, clove and peppercorn. Heat gently, stirring occasionally, until the sugar has dissolved.

Meanwhile, peel the pears, leaving the core and stem intact on each. Slice a small piece off the base of each pear so that it will stand upright, then gently place the pears in the wine mixture. Simmer the pears uncovered, for 20–35 minutes, depending on size and ripeness. They should be just tender; do not overcook.

With a slotted spoon, gently transfer the pears to a bowl. Continue to boil the poaching liquid until reduced by about half. Let cool, then strain over the pears. Chill for at least 3 hours.

Place the pears in serving dishes and spoon the chilled wine syrup over them. Serve with whipped or sour cream.

COOK'S TIP
Choose pears of similar size and shape for this attractive hot dessert.

FRUDITÉS WITH HONEY DIP

Some of the simplest desserts are also the most delectable. This takes only minutes to make but tastes absolutely wonderful, making use of the classic honey and yogurt combination.

Serves 4

250ml/8fl oz/1 cup thick natural
    yogurt
45ml/3 tbsp clear honey
selection of fresh fruit for dipping
    (such as apples, pears, tangerines,
    grapes, figs, cherries, strawberries
    and kiwi fruit)

VARIATION
Add a few langues de chat or other dessert biscuits, such as sponge fingers, to the platter. Children like the yogurt dip served on its own, with sliced bananas stirred in.

Place the yogurt in a dish, beat until smooth, then stir in the honey, swirling it to create a marbled effect.

Cut the fruit into wedges or bite-size pieces, or leave whole.

Arrange the selection of fruits on a platter with the bowl of dip in the centre. Serve chilled.

BRAZILIAN COFFEE BANANAS

Rich, lavish, and sinful-looking, this banana dessert takes only moments to make!

Serves 4

4 small ripe bananas

*1 tbsp instant coffee granules
  or powder*

2 tbsp dark brown sugar

*generous 1 cup Greek-
  style yogurt*

1 tbsp toasted slivered almonds

VARIATION

*For a special occasion, add a
dash of dark rum or brandy, or
crème de cacao to the bananas
for extra richness.*

Peel and slice one banana. Peel and mash the remaining three in a bowl with a fork. Dissolve the coffee in 1 tbsp boiling water and stir into the mashed bananas.

Spoon a little of the mashed banana mixture into four serving dishes and sprinkle with sugar. Top with a spoonful of yogurt, then repeat the layers until all the ingredients are used up.

Using a skewer or toothpick, swirl the last layer of yogurt for a marbled effect. Finish with a few banana slices and slivered almonds. Serve cold, preferably within an hour of making.

APPLE FOAM WITH BLACKBERRIES

Any seasonal berry can be used for this delicious dessert if blackberries are not available at the time.

Serves 4

2 cups blackberries
2/3 cup apple juice
1 teaspoon powdered gelatin
1 tablespoon clear honey
2 egg whites

COOK'S TIP
Make sure that you add the gelatin to a cold liquid before dissolving over very low heat. Gelatin must not boil, or it will lose its setting ability. Once set, gelatin mixtures should be chilled for about 2 hours to become firm. Don't be tempted to chill a gelatin mixture quickly in the freezer, as it tends to crystallize and separate.

Place the blackberries in a pan with 4 tablespoons of the apple juice and heat gently until the fruit is soft. Remove from the heat, cool and chill.

Sprinkle the gelatin over the remaining apple juice in a small pan and stir over low heat until dissolved. Stir in the honey.

Whisk the egg whites until they hold stiff peaks. Continue whisking hard and pour in the hot gelatin mixture gradually, until well mixed.

Quickly spoon the foam into rough mounds on individual plates. Chill. Serve with the blackberries and juice spooned around.

PEACHES WITH RASPBERRY SAUCE

Escoffier created this dessert, known as Peach Melba, in honor of the opera singer Nellie Melba.

Serves 6

4 cups water

¼ cup superfine sugar

1 vanilla bean, split lengthwise

3 large peaches, halved and pitted

For the raspberry sauce

2½ cups fresh or frozen raspberries

1 tablespoon lemon juice

2–3 tablespoons superfine sugar

*2–3 tablespoons raspberry
   liqueur (optional)*

vanilla ice cream, to serve

mint leaves, to decorate

COOK'S TIP

*Prepare the peaches and sauce
up to one day in advance. Leave
the peaches in the syrup and
cover them and the sauce
before chilling.*

In a large saucepan, combine the water, sugar and vanilla bean. Bring to a boil, stirring to dissolve the sugar. Add the peaches, cut-sides down, and water, if needed, to cover the fruit. Press a piece of wax paper against the surface, then cover and simmer for 12–15 minutes until tender. Remove the pan from the heat and let the peaches cool. Peel the peaches.

Process the raspberries, lemon juice and sugar in a food processor for 1 minute then strain into a bowl. Add the raspberry liqueur, if using, and chill. To serve, place a peach half, cut-side up, add vanilla ice cream and spoon over the raspberry sauce. Decorate with mint leaves.

RASPBERRY AND PASSIONFRUIT PUFFS

Few desserts are as easy to make as this one: beaten egg whites and sugar baked in a dish, turned out and served with a handful of raspberries.

Serves 4

2 tablespoons butter, softened

5 egg whites

⅔ cup superfine sugar

2 passionfruits

1 cup ready-made custard sauce from a carton or can

milk, as required

4 cups fresh raspberries

confectioner's sugar, for dusting

Preheat the oven to 350°F. Brush four 1¼-cup soufflé dishes with a visible layer of soft butter.

Whisk the egg whites in a mixing bowl until firm. (You can use an electric whisk). Add the sugar a little at a time and whisk into a firm meringue.

Halve the passionfruits, take out the seeds with a spoon and fold them into the meringue.

Spoon the meringue into the prepared dishes, stand in a deep roasting pan which has been half-filled with boiling water and bake for 10 minutes. The meringue will rise above the tops of the soufflé dishes.

Turn out the puffs upside-down on to serving plates. Thin the custard sauce with a little milk and pour around the edge. Top with raspberries, dredge with confectioner's sugar and serve warm or cold.

VARIATION

If raspberries are out of season, use either fresh, bottled or canned soft berry fruits such as strawberries, blueberries, blackberries or red currants.

FLUFFY BANANA AND PINEAPPLE MOUSSE

This light, low-fat banana mousse looks very impressive but is very easy to make.

Serves 6

2 ripe bananas

1 cup cottage cheese

15oz can pineapple chunks or pieces in juice

1 sachet powdered gelatin

2 egg whites

COOK'S TIP

For a simpler way of serving, use a 4-cup serving dish, which is able to hold all the mixture, and do not tie a collar around the top edge. Decorate the top of the mousse with the reserved banana and pineapple as described in the recipe.

Tie a double band of baking parchment around a 2½-cup soufflé dish, to come 2in above the rim. Peel and chop one banana and place it in a food processor with the cottage cheese. Process until smooth.

Drain the pineapple, saving the juice, and setting aside a few pieces for decoration. Add the rest of the pineapple to the mixture in the processor and process for a few seconds until finely chopped.

Pour 4 tbsp of the reserved pineapple juice into a small heatproof bowl and sprinkle the gelatin on top. When spongy, place over simmering water, stirring until the gelatin has dissolved. Stir the gelatin quickly into the fruit mixture. Whisk the egg whites to soft peaks. Fold them into the mixture. Tip the mousse mixture into the prepared dish, smooth the surface, and chill until set. Carefully remove the paper collar. Slice the remaining banana and use it with the reserved pineapple to decorate the mousse.

MANGO AND GINGER CLOUDS

The sweet, perfumed flavor of ripe mango combines beautifully with ginger, and this low-fat dessert makes the very most of them both.

Serves 6

3 ripe mangoes

3 pieces preserved ginger in syrup

3 tablespoons preserved ginger syrup

½ cup silken tofu

3 egg whites

6 pistachios, chopped

Cut the mangoes in half and remove the pits. Peel and coarsely chop the flesh. Put the mango flesh in a blender or food processor, with the preserved ginger, ginger syrup and tofu. Blend the mixture until smooth, then spoon into a bowl. Put the egg whites in a bowl and whisk them until they form soft peaks. Fold them lightly into the mango mixture. Spoon the mixture into wide dishes or glasses and chill before serving, sprinkled with the chopped pistachios.

VARIATION

If you prefer, you can serve this dessert lightly frozen. Add the nuts just before serving.

COOK'S TIP

Don't serve raw egg whites to pregnant women, babies, young children, the elderly, or anyone who is ill.

GRAPE AND HONEY WHIP

Frosted grapes add the finishing touches to this simple dessert, which is sweetened with clear honey.

Serves 4

1 cup black or green seedless grapes,
    plus 4 sprigs

2 egg whites

1 tablespoon sugar

finely grated rind and juice of
    ½ lemon

1 cup cream cheese

3 tablespoons clear honey

2 tablespoons brandy (optional)

VARIATION
Instead of brandy, use a honey-based liqueur such as Irish Mist, made from Irish whiskey, heather honey and herbs.

Brush the sprigs of grapes lightly with some of the egg whites and sprinkle with sugar to coat. Let dry.

Pour the lemon juice into a bowl and stir in the lemon rind, cheese, honey and brandy, if using. Chop the remaining grapes and stir them in.

Whisk the remaining egg whites until they are stiff enough to hold soft peaks. Fold them into the grape mixture, then spoon into serving glasses. Top with the sugar-frosted grapes and serve chilled.

RASPBERRY AND PASSIONFRUIT SWIRLS

If passionfruits are not available, this simple low-fat dessert can be made with raspberries alone.

Serves 4

2 cups raspberries

2 passionfruits

1⅔ cups low-fat plain yogurt

2 tablespoons sugar

raspberries and mint sprigs, to decorate

Mash the raspberries in a small bowl with a fork until the juice runs. Scoop out the passionfruit pulp into a separate bowl with the yogurt and sugar and mix well.

Spoon alternate spoonfuls of the raspberry pulp and the yogurt mixture into stemmed glasses or one large serving dish, stirring lightly to create a swirled effect.

Decorate each dessert with a whole raspberry and a fresh mint sprig. Chill until ready to serve.

COOK'S TIP
Over-ripe, slightly soft fruit can also be used in this recipe. Use frozen raspberries when fresh ones are not available, but thaw them first.

QUICK BANANA PUDDING

For instant energy and excellent taste, enjoy this simple banana pudding with a caramel topping.

Serves 6–8

4 thick slices of ginger cake

6 ripe bananas

2 tbsp lemon juice

1¼ cups heavy cream

4 tbsp orange juice

2–3 tbsp brown sugar

VARIATION

Use fromage frais instead of heavy cream if you prefer. However, do not try to whip it – just stir in half the recommended amount of fruit juice.

Break up the cake into chunks and arrange in an ovenproof dish. Slice the bananas into a bowl and toss with the lemon juice.

Whip the cream in a separate bowl until firm, then gently beat in the juice. Fold in the bananas and spoon the mixture over the ginger cake.

Top with the sugar, sprinkling it in an even layer. Place under a hot broiler for 2–3 minutes to caramelize. Chill in the refrigerator until set firm again if you wish, or serve at once.

BANANA AND PASSION FRUIT WHIP

Creamy mashed bananas combine beautifully with passion fruit in this easy and quickly prepared dessert.

Serves 4

2 ripe bananas

2 passion fruit

6 tbsp fromage frais

⅔ cup heavy cream

2 tsp clear honey

shortcake or ginger cookies, to serve

COOK'S TIP

Look out for cans of passion fruit (or grenadilla) pulp. Use with sliced banana and whipped cream to make a marvelous topping for pavlova or for sandwiching together individual meringues.

Slice the bananas into a bowl, then, using a fork, mash them to a smooth purée. Cut the passion fruit in half. Using a teaspoon, scoop the pulp into the bowl. Add the fromage frais and mix gently. In a separate bowl, whip the cream with the honey until it forms soft peaks. Carefully fold the cream and honey mixture into the fruit. Spoon into four glass dishes and serve the whip at once, with the cookies.

BLACKBERRY AND APPLE ROMANOFF

Rich yet fruity, this dessert is popular with most people and very quick to make.

Serves 6–8

3–4 sharp eating apples, peeled, cored
    and chopped

3 tablespoons superfine sugar

1 cup whipping cream

1 teaspoon grated lemon rind

6 tablespoons strained plain yogurt

4–6 crisp meringues (about 2 ounces),
    coarsely crumbled

8 ounces fresh or frozen blackberries

whipped cream, a few blackberries,
    and mint leaves, to decorate

COOK'S TIP

*This also makes a delicious ice
cream, though the texture of the
frozen berries makes it difficult
to scoop if it is frozen for more
than 4–6 hours.*

With plastic wrap, line a 4–5-cup pudding bowl. Toss the apples into a pan with 2 tablespoons of the sugar and cook for 2–3 minutes, or until softening. Mash the apples with a fork and let cool.

Whip the cream and fold in the lemon rind, yogurt, the remaining sugar, the apples, and the crumbled meringues.

Gently stir in the blackberries, then tip the mixture into the pudding bowl and freeze for 1–3 hours.

Turn out on to a plate and remove the plastic wrap. Serve decorated with piped cream, blackberries, and mint leaves.

BANANA HONEY YOGURT ICE

Smooth and silky, this delicious banana ice is very refreshing when eaten after a rich meal.

Serves 4–6

4 ripe bananas, roughly chopped

1 tbsp lemon juice

2 tbsp clear honey

generous 1 cup Greek-
*   style yogurt*

½ tsp ground cinnamon

crisp cookies, flaked hazelnuts, and
*   banana slices, to serve*

Place the bananas in a food processor or blender with the lemon juice, honey, yogurt, and cinnamon. Process until smooth and creamy.

Pour the mixture into a suitable container for freezing and freeze until almost solid. Spoon back into the food processor and process the mixture again until smooth.

Return the yogurt ice to the freezer until firm. Before serving, allow the ice to soften at room temperature for 15 minutes. Scoop into individual bowls and serve with crisp cookies, flaked hazelnuts, and banana slices.

COOK'S TIP

Switch the freezer to the coldest
setting about an hour before
making the yogurt ice to ensure
that it freezes quickly.

BREAD AND BANANA YOGURT ICE

Serve this tempting yogurt ice with strawberries and cookies, for a luscious and light dessert.

Serves 6

*2 cups fresh whole wheat
    breadcrumbs*

⅓ cup brown sugar

1¾ cups ready-made cold custard

5oz fromage frais

*⅔ cup Greek-style
    yogurt*

4 bananas

juice of 1 lemon

¼ cup confectioner's sugar, sifted

½ cup raisins, chopped

pared lemon rind, to decorate

*fresh strawberries, halved, to serve
    (optional)*

Preheat the oven to 400°F. Mix the breadcrumbs and brown sugar in a bowl. Spread the mixture out on a non-stick cookie sheet. Bake for about 10 minutes until the crumbs are crisp, stirring occasionally. Set aside to cool.

Meanwhile, mix the custard, fromage frais, and yogurt in a bowl. Mash the bananas with the lemon juice and add to the custard mixture, mixing well. Fold in the confectioner's sugar.

Pour the mixture into a shallow, freezerproof container and freeze for about 3 hours or until mushy in consistency. Spoon into a chilled bowl and quickly mash with a fork to break down the ice crystals.

Add the breadcrumbs and raisins and mix well. Return the mixture to the container, cover, and freeze until firm. Serve with the strawberries, if using, decorated with lemon rind.

COOK'S TIP

Transfer the ice to the refrigerator about 30 minutes before serving to allow it to soften a little. This will make it easier to scoop neatly so that it looks attractive when served.

FROZEN APPLE AND BLACKBERRY TERRINE

Apples and blackberries are a classic seasonal combination; they really complement each other. This pretty, three-layered terrine can be frozen, so you can enjoy it at any time of year.

Serves 6

2 cooking or eating apples (about 1 pound)

1¼ cups cider

1 tablespoon clear honey

1 teaspoon vanilla extract

scant 2 cups fresh or frozen blackberries, thawed

1 packet powdered gelatin

2 egg whites

fresh apple slices and blackberries, to decorate

COOK'S TIP

For a quicker version, set the mixture without layering. Purée the fruit together, stir in the dissolved gelatin and whisked egg whites, turn into the pan and let set.

Peel, core, and chop the apples and place them in a pan, with half the cider. Bring the cider to a boil, then cover the pan and let the apples simmer gently until tender.

Turn the apples into a food processor or blender and process to a smooth purée. Stir in the honey and vanilla. Add half the blackberries to half the apple purée. Process again until smooth. Strain to remove the seeds.

Heat the remaining cider until it is almost boiling, and then sprinkle the gelatin over and stir until the gelatin has completely dissolved. Add half the gelatin mixture to the apple purée and half to the blackberry purée.

Let the purées cool until almost set. Whisk the egg whites until they are stiff. Quickly fold them into the apple purée. Remove half the purée to another bowl. Stir the remaining whole blackberries into half the apple purée, and then turn this into a 7½-cup loaf pan, packing it down firmly.

Top with the blackberry purée and spread it evenly. Finally, add a layer of the apple purée and smooth it evenly. If necessary, freeze each layer until firm before adding the next.

Freeze until firm. To serve, allow to stand at room temperature for about 20 minutes to soften, and then cut into slices, decorated with the fresh apple slices and some blackberries.

MINT AND LEMON SORBET

This sorbet has a very refreshing, delicate taste, perfect for a hot afternoon.

Serves 6–8

2 cups sugar

2 cups water

6 mint sprigs, plus more to decorate

6 lemon balm leaves

1 cup dry white wine

2 tablespoons lemon juice

dill sprigs, to decorate

Place the sugar and water in a saucepan with the washed herbs. Bring to a boil. Remove from the heat and add the wine. Cover and cool. Chill for several hours, then add the lemon juice. Freeze in a suitable container. As soon as the mixture begins to freeze, stir it briskly and replace in the freezer. Repeat every 15 minutes for at least 3 hours or until ready to serve.

To make the small ice bowls, pour about ½ inch cold, boiled water into small freezer-proof bowls, about 2½ cups in capacity, and arrange some herbs in the water. Place in the freezer. Once this has frozen add a little more water to cover the herbs and freeze.

Place a smaller freezer-proof bowl inside each larger bowl and put a heavy weight inside, such as a metal weight from scales. Fill between the bowls with more cooled boiled water, float more herbs in this and freeze.

To release the ice bowls, warm the inner bowl with a small amount of very hot water and twist it out. Warm the outer bowl by standing it in very hot water for a few seconds, then tip out the ice bowl. Spoon the sorbet into the ice bowls, decorate with mint and dill sprigs and serve.

COOK'S TIP

In place of lemon balm leaves, fresh flowers can be used in the ice bowl. Small pansies, marigolds or geraniums would all be suitable.

BLACKBERRY SALAD WITH ROSE GRANITA

The blackberries combine especially well with rose water. Here a rose syrup is frozen into a granita and served over strips of white meringue.

Serves 4
2/3 cup superfine sugar
1 fresh red rose, petals finely chopped
1 teaspoon rose water
2 teaspoons lemon juice
4 cups blackberries
confectioner's sugar, for dusting

For the meringue
2 egg whites
1/2 cup superfine sugar

COOK'S TIP
Blackberries are widely cultivated from late spring to fall and are usually juicy, plump and sweet. The finest berries have a slightly bitter edge and a strong depth of flavor. They are best appreciated with a light sprinkling of sugar.

Bring 2/3 cup water to a boil in a stainless-steel or enamel saucepan. Add the sugar and rose petals, then simmer for 5 minutes. Strain the syrup into a deep metal tray, add a scant 2 cups more water, the rose water and lemon juice, and leave to cool. Freeze the mixture for 3 hours or until solid.

Preheat the oven to 275°F. Line a cookie sheet with 6 layers of newspaper and cover with buttered waxed paper.

To make the meringue, whisk the egg whites until they hold soft peaks. Add the superfine sugar a little at a time and whisk until firm.

Spoon the meringue into a pastry bag fitted with a 1/2-inch plain nozzle. Pipe the meringue in lengths across the lined cookie sheet. Bake in the bottom of the oven for 1 1/2–2 hours.

Break the meringue into 2-inch lengths and place three or four lengths on each of four large plates. Pile the blackberries next to the meringue. With a tablespoon, scrape the granita finely. Shape into ovals and place over the meringue. Dust with confectioner's sugar and serve.

LEMON MERINGUE BOMBE WITH MINT CHOCOLATE

This unusual ice cream has quite the most delicious combination of tastes that you can imagine.

Serves 6–8

2 large lemons

⅔ cup sugar

⅔ cup whipping cream

2½ cups strained plain yogurt

2 large meringues, roughly crushed

3 small mint sprigs

8 ounces good-quality mint chocolate, grated

Remove the rind from the lemons with a vegetable peeler, then squeeze the juice. Place the lemon rind and sugar in a blender or food processor and blend finely. Add the cream, yogurt and lemon juice and process thoroughly. Pour the mixture into a mixing bowl and add the meringues.

Reserve one of the mint sprigs for decoration and chop the rest finely. Add to the cream and lemon mixture. Pour the mixture into a 5-cup glass bowl and freeze for about 4 hours.

When the ice cream has frozen, scoop out the middle and pour in the grated mint chocolate, reserving a little for the garnish. Replace the ice cream to cover the chocolate and refreeze.

To unmold, dip the bowl in very hot water for a few seconds to loosen the ice cream, then invert the bowl over a serving plate. Decorate with grated chocolate and a mint sprig.

COOK'S TIP

If you prefer, use either milk or plain chocolate in place of mint chocolate. To make a richer ice cream, use cream in place of the strained plain yogurt.

COFFEE, PEACH, AND ALMOND DAQUOISE

This is a traditional meringue cake, filled with a rich coffee buttercream and layered with peaches.

Serves 12

5 egg whites

1¼ cups superfine sugar

2 tablespoons cornstarch

1½ cups ground almonds, toasted

For the custard

5 egg yolks

¾ cup superfine sugar

generous ½ cup milk

1¼ cups sweet butter, diced

3–4 tablespoons coffee essence

2 × 14-ounce cans peach halves, drained and chopped, 3 halves reserved for decoration

confectioner's sugar, for dusting

toasted slivered almonds and a few mint leaves, to decorate

Preheat the oven to 300°F and draw three 9-inch circles on three sheets of nonstick baking parchment. Place each on a separate cookie sheet. Whisk the egg whites until stiff and gradually add the sugar, whisking until the mixture is thick and glossy. Fold in the cornstarch and ground almonds. Spoon the mixture into a pastry bag fitted with a plain tip and pipe in a continuous tight coil onto each prepared piece of baking parchment, starting at the center and gradually filling the circle. Bake for 1¾–2 hours, until lightly golden and dried out. Peel off the parchment and cool on a wire rack.

Make the custard: whisk the egg yolks with the sugar until thick and pale. Heat the milk in a pan until nearly boiling and pour into the egg mixture. Return the mixture to the pan and cook over low heat until just thickened. Cool slightly and strain into a bowl. Beat in the butter, a little at a time, until thickened and stir in the coffee essence.

Trim the meringue neatly, crushing any trimmings. Fold the chopped peaches and meringue trimmings into half of the custard and use this to sandwich the meringue rounds together. Coat the top and sides of the meringue with the remaining custard and decorate with toasted slivered almond. Dust with confectioner's sugar and finish with fans of the reserved peaches and a few mint leaves.

RASPBERRY MERINGUE GATEAU

A crisp, rich, hazelnut meringue filled with whipped cream and raspberries makes a wonderful dessert served with a fresh raspberry and orange sauce.

Serves 6

4 egg whites

1 cup sugar

few drops vanilla extract

1 teaspoon distilled malt vinegar

1 cup roasted and chopped
  hazelnuts, ground

1¼ cups heavy cream

2 cups raspberries

confectioner's sugar, for dusting

raspberries and mint sprigs, to decorate

For the sauce

1⅓ cups raspberries

3–4 tablespoons confectioner's
  sugar, sifted

1 tablespoon orange liqueur

VARIATION

Fresh red currants make a good alternative to raspberries. Add to the cream with a little sugar.

Preheat the oven to 350°F. Grease two 8-inch shallow cake pans and line the bases with rounds of wax paper.

Whisk the egg whites in a large bowl until they hold stiff peaks, then gradually whisk in the sugar a tablespoon at a time, whisking well after each addition.

Continue whisking the meringue mixture for a minute or two until very stiff, then fold in the vanilla extract, vinegar and ground hazelnuts.

Divide the meringue mixture between the prepared cake pans and spread level. Bake for 50–60 minutes, until crisp. Remove the meringues from the pans and leave to cool on a wire rack.

While the meringues are cooling, make the sauce. Purée the raspberries with the confectioner's sugar and orange liqueur in a blender or food processor, then press the purée through a fine nylon strainer to remove any seeds. Chill the sauce until ready to serve.

Whip the cream until it forms soft peaks, then gently fold in the raspberries. Sandwich the meringue rounds together with the raspberry cream. Dust the top of the gâteau with confectioner's sugar. Decorate with raspberries and mint sprigs and serve with the raspberry sauce.

BLACKBERRY BROWN SUGAR MERINGUE

Brown sugar gives this meringue a delicate, fudge-like flavor which combines well with the berry filling.

Serves 6

1 cup soft light brown sugar

3 egg whites

1 teaspoon distilled malt vinegar

½ teaspoon vanilla extract

For the filling

3 cups blackberries

2 tablespoons black currant liqueur

1¼ cups heavy cream

1 tablespoons confectioner's
* sugar, sifted*

blackberry leaves, to decorate
* (optional)*

Preheat the oven to 325°F. Draw an 8-inch circle on a sheet of wax paper, then turn it over and place on a cookie sheet. Set aside.

Spread out the brown sugar on another cookie sheet and dry in the oven for 8–10 minutes. Rub through a strainer to remove any lumps.

Whisk the egg whites in a bowl until stiff. Add half the dried brown sugar, 1 tablespoon at a time, whisking well after each addition. Add the vinegar and vanilla extract, then fold in the remaining sugar.

Spoon the meringue on to the drawn circle on the paper, leaving a hollow in the center. Bake for 45 minutes, then turn off the oven and leave the meringue in the oven with the door slightly open, until cold.

Place the blackberries in a bowl, sprinkle over the liqueur and leave to macerate for 30 minutes.

When the meringue is cold, carefully peel off the wax paper and transfer the meringue to a serving plate. Lightly whip the cream with the confectioner's sugar and spoon into the center. Top with the blackberries and decorate with small blackberry leaves, if liked. Serve the meringue at once.

RASPBERRY AND NECTARINE PAVLOVA

This meringue was created in the 1920s for the ballerina Anna Pavlova, when she visited Australia.

Serves 4–6

3 egg whites

¾ cup superfine sugar

1 teaspoon cornstarch

1 teaspoon white wine vinegar

5 tablespoons chopped hazelnuts, roasted

1 cup heavy cream

1 tablespoon orange juice

2 tablespoons thick and creamy plain yogurt

2 ripe nectarines, pitted and sliced

1⅓ cups raspberries, halved

1–2 tablespoons red currant or raspberry jelly, warmed

Preheat the oven to 275°F. Lightly grease a cookie sheet. Draw an 8-inch circle on a sheet of parchment paper. Place pencil-side down on the greased cookie sheet.

Place the egg whites in a clean, grease-free bowl and whisk with an electric mixer until stiff. Whisk in the sugar, 1 tablespoon at a time, whisking well after each addition. Add the cornstarch, vinegar and hazelnuts and fold in carefully with a large metal spoon. Spoon the meringue on to the marked circle and spread out to the edges, making a dip in the center. Bake for about 1¼–1½ hours, until crisp. Leave to cool completely and transfer to a serving platter. Whip the cream and orange juice until just thick, stir in the yogurt and spoon on to the meringue. Top with the fruit and drizzle over the warmed jelly. Serve immediately.

HONEY AND MANGO CHEESECAKE

Use a fragrant citrus honey to complement the mango and lime in this exotic cheesecake.

Serves 4

3 tablespoons butter or margarine,
    softened

2 tablespoons clear honey

2 cups oatmeal

1 large ripe mango, peeled, pitted
    and roughly chopped

1¼ cups cream cheese

¾ cup plain yogurt

finely grated rind of 1 small lime

3 tablespoons apple juice

4 teaspoons powdered gelatin

fresh mango and lime slices, to
    decorate

VARIATION

Use drained canned mango slices instead of fresh, if you prefer, but add a few drops of fresh lime juice to counteract the sweetness.

Preheat the oven to 400°F. Cream the butter with the honey in a bowl, then stir in the oatmeal. Press the mixture into the base of an 8-inch springform cake pan. Bake for 12–15 minutes, until lightly browned. Cool.

Place the chopped mango, cheese, yogurt and lime rind in a food processor or blender and process until smooth.

Put the apple juice in a small heatproof bowl and sprinkle the gelatine on top. When spongy, set over simmering water and stir until the gelatin has dissolved. Stir into the cheese mixture.

Pour the filling over the cheesecake base and chill until set, then remove from the pan and place on a serving plate. Decorate the top with the mango and lime slices.

LEMON CHEESECAKE ON BRANDY SNAPS

Using ready-made brandy snaps gives a quick and crunchy golden base to this simple and delicious classic lemon cheesecake.

Serves 8

1 package lemon jello

2 cups low-fat cream cheese

2 teaspoons lemon rind

about ½ cup superfine sugar

few drops vanilla extract

⅔ cup strained plain yogurt

8 brandy snaps

mint leaves and confectioner's sugar,
* to decorate*

Dissolve the jello in 3–4 tablespoons boiling water in a heatproof measuring cup and, when clear, add sufficient cold water to make up to ⅔ cup, stirring well to mix. Chill the jello until beginning to thicken. Line a 1-pound loaf pan with plastic wrap.

Cream the cheese with the lemon rind, sugar and vanilla and beat until light and smooth. Then fold in the thickening lemon jello and the yogurt. Spoon into the prepared pan and chill until set. Preheat the oven to 325°F.

Place two or three brandy snaps at a time on a cookie sheet. Place in the oven for no more than 1 minute, until soft enough to unroll and flatten out completely. Leave on a cold plate or tray to harden again. Repeat with the remaining brandy snaps.

To serve, turn the cheesecake out on to a board with the help of the plastic wrap. Cut into eight slices and place one slice on each brandy snap base. Decorate with mint leaves and sprinkle with confectioner's sugar.

COOK'S TIP

If you don't have any brandy snaps to hand, you could serve this cheesecake on thin slices of moist ginger cake, or on other thin, crisp cookies.

APPLE AND HAZELNUT SHORTCAKE

This variation of a traditional recipe will be popular with all the family.

Serves 8–10

1 cup whole wheat flour

4 tablespoons ground hazelnuts

4 tablespoons confectioner's
sugar, sifted

10 tablespoons sweet butter
or margarine

3 sharp eating apples

1 teaspoon lemon juice

about 1–2 tablespoons sugar, to taste

1 tablespoon chopped fresh mint, or
1 teaspoon dried

1 cup whipping cream or crème fraîche

few drops of vanilla extract

few mint leaves and whole hazelnuts,
to decorate

Process the flour, ground hazelnuts, and confectioner's sugar with the butter in a food processor or blender in short bursts, or rub the butter into the dry ingredients until they come together into a ball. (Don't overwork the mixture.) Add a very little iced water if necessary. Knead briefly, then chill, covered or wrapped, for about 30 minutes.

Preheat the oven to 325°F. Cut the chilled dough in half and roll out each half, on a lightly floured surface, to form a 7-inch round. Place the rounds on wax paper on baking sheets and bake for about 40 minutes, or until crisp. If the shortcakes are browning too much, move them down in the oven to a lower shelf. Allow to cool.

Peel, core, and chop the apples into a pan with the lemon juice. Add sugar to taste, then cook for about 2–3 minutes, until just softening. Mash the apple gently with the chopped fresh mint and let cool.

Whip the cream or crème fraîche with the vanilla extract. Place one shortcake round on a serving plate. Carefully spread half the apple and then half the cream or crème fraîche on top of the shortcake.

Place the second shortcake on top, then spread over the remaining apple and cream, swirling the top layer of cream gently. Serve immediately decorated with mint leaves and a few whole hazelnuts.

LEMON MERINGUE PIE

A classic, popular pie with a piquant filling and golden meringue topping.

Serves 6–8

1⅓ cups superfine sugar

¼ cup cornstarch

pinch of salt

2 tablespoons finely grated lemon rind

½ cup fresh lemon juice

1 cup water

3 eggs, separated

3 tablespoons butter

9-inch pie shell

pinch of cream of tartar (if needed)

COOK'S TIP

Egg whites can be beaten to their greatest volume if they are at room temperature rather than cold. A copper bowl and wire balloon whisk are the best tools to use, although a stainless-steel bowl and electric mixer produce very good results. Take care not to overbeat whites (they will look grainy and separate).

Combine 1 cup sugar, the cornstarch, salt, and lemon rind in a saucepan. Stir in the lemon juice and water until smoothly blended.

Bring to a boil over medium-high heat, stirring constantly. Simmer until the mixture is thickened, about 1 minute.

Blend in the egg yolks. Cook the mixture over medium-low heat about 2 minutes more, stirring constantly.

Remove the saucepan from the heat. Add the butter and mix well.

Pour the lemon filling into the prepared pie shell. Spread the filling evenly and smooth the surface with a spatula. Let cool completely.

Preheat the oven to 350°F.

In a scrupulously clean, grease-free bowl, beat the egg whites until they will hold soft peaks. (If not using a copper bowl, add the cream of tartar as soon as the whites are frothy). Add the remaining sugar and continue beating until the mixture is stiff and glossy.

Spread the meringue evenly over the filling with a spatula. Take care to seal it to the edges of the pie shell all around.

Bake until the meringue is just set and lightly golden brown on the surface, 10–15 minutes. Let cool before serving.

BOSTON BANOFFEE PIE

Guaranteed to bring a grin to diners' faces, this is a winning combination of bananas and toffee.

Makes an 8in pie

8in cooked pastry case, cooled

2 small bananas, sliced

a little lemon juice

*whipped cream and grated dark
   chocolate, to decorate*

For the filling

½ cup butter

*½ x 14oz can sweetened condensed
   milk*

⅔ cup brown sugar

2 tbsp corn syrup

COOK'S TIP

*To make the pastry case, rub
½ cup butter into 1¼ cups all-
purpose flour. Stir in 4 tbsp
superfine sugar and press into
an 8in flan pan. Line the
dough case with crumpled foil
or baking beans. Bake at
325°F for 20–25 minutes.*

Make the filling. Place the butter, condensed milk, brown sugar, and corn syrup in a large non-stick saucepan. Heat gently, stirring occasionally, until the sugar has dissolved.

Bring to a gentle boil and cook for 7 minutes, stirring all the time (to prevent burning), until the mixture thickens and turns a light caramel color. Pour into the cooked pastry case and leave until cold.

Decorate with the bananas dipped in the lemon juice. Pipe a swirl of whipped cream in the center and sprinkle with the grated chocolate.

SUMMER FRUIT DESSERT

This is a classic English dessert, traditionally made in midsummer.

Serves 4

about 8 thin slices day-old white bread,
  crusts removed

1¾ pounds mixed berries

about 2 tablespoons sugar

Cut a round from one slice of bread to fit in the base of a 5-cup mixing bowl, then cut strips of bread about 2 inches wide to line the bowl, overlapping the strips slightly.

Gently heat the berries, sugar and 2 tablespoons water in a large heavy saucepan, shaking the pan occasionally, until the juices begin to run.

Reserve about 3 tablespoons fruit juice, then spoon the fruit and remaining juice into the bowl, taking care not to dislodge the bread.

Cut the remaining bread to cover the fruit. Stand the bowl on a plate and cover with a saucer or plate that will just fit inside the top of the bowl. Place a heavy weight on top. Chill the dessert and reserved fruit juice overnight.

Run a knife carefully around the inside of the bowl rim, then invert the dessert on to a cold serving plate. Pour over the reserved juice and serve.

COOK'S TIP
Use a selection of soft, juicy berries such as red currants, raspberries and blackberries.

hot desserts

Apple pies often spring to mind at the mention of hot fruit desserts, but bananas, pears, citrus fruits and various berries are equally versatile and make a valuable contribution to the repertoire of dishes. Simple and speedy recipes include scrumptious Hot Bananas with Rum and Raisins, glistening Red Berry Tart with Lemon Cream Filling and an extra special Apple Couscous Pudding.

SPICED NUTTY BANANAS

Baked bananas are delectable however you serve them, but with a triple nut topping they are delicious.

Serves 3

6 ripe, but firm, bananas

2 tbsp chopped unsalted
   cashew nuts

2 tbsp chopped unsalted
   peanuts

2 tbsp shredded coconut

1 tbsp brown sugar

1 tsp ground cinnamon

½ tsp freshly grated nutmeg

⅔ cup orange juice

4 tbsp rum

1 tbsp butter or margarine

heavy cream or Greek-style yogurt,
   to serve

COOK'S TIP

*Freshly grated nutmeg makes
all the difference to this dish.
More rum can be added if
preferred. Chopped mixed nuts
can be used instead of peanuts.*

Preheat the oven to 400°F. Slice the bananas and place in a large, greased, shallow ovenproof dish. Do not leave for long at this stage as the bananas will discolor.

Mix the cashew nuts, peanuts, coconut, sugar, cinnamon, and nutmeg in a small bowl. Pour the orange juice and rum over the bananas, then sprinkle evenly with the nut and sugar mixture.

Dot the top evenly with butter or margarine. Bake for 15–20 minutes or until the bananas are golden brown and the sauce is bubbling.

Serve the bananas hot, with heavy cream or Greek-style yogurt.

KUMQUAT AND HONEY COMPOTE

Sun-ripened, warm and spicy ingredients, sweetened with honey, make the perfect winter dessert.

Serves 4

350g/12oz/2 cups kumquats

275g/10oz/1¼ cups dried apricots

30ml/2 tbsp raisins

30ml/2 tbsp lemon juice

1 orange

2.5cm/1in piece of fresh root ginger

4 cardamom pods

4 cloves

30ml/2 tbsp clear honey

15ml/1 tbsp flaked almonds, toasted,
  to decorate

VARIATION

If you prefer, use ready-to-eat dried apricots. Reduce the liquid to 300ml/½pint/1¼cups, and add the apricots for the last 5 minutes of cooking.

Wash the kumquats, and, if they are large, cut them in half. Place them in a large saucepan with the dried apricots and raisins. Pour over 300ml/½ pint/1¼ cups water and add the lemon juice. Bring to the boil.

Pare the rind thinly from the orange and add to the pan. Peel the ginger, grate it finely and add it to the pan. Lightly crush the cardamom pods and add them to the pan, with the cloves.

Lower the heat, cover the pan and simmer gently for about 30 minutes or until the fruit is tender, stirring occasionally.

Squeeze the juice from the orange and add it to the pan with the honey. Stir well, then taste and add more honey if required. Sprinkle with flaked almonds and serve warm.

BANANA MANDAZIS

These delicious banana fritters come from Africa, where they are very popular.

Serves 4

1 egg

2 ripe bananas, roughly chopped

⅔ cup milk

½ tsp vanilla extract

2 cups self-rising flour

1 tsp baking powder

3 tbsp sugar

vegetable oil, for deep-frying

confectioner's sugar, for dusting

COOK'S TIP

Drain each batch of mandazis well on paper towels and keep them hot in a low oven while you are cooking the remainder.

Place the egg, bananas, milk, vanilla extract, flour, baking powder, and sugar in a blender or food processor. Process to a smooth, creamy batter. If it is too thick, add a little extra milk. Set aside for 10 minutes.

Heat the oil in a heavy-based saucepan or deep-fat fryer. When it is hot, place spoonfuls of the mixture in the oil and fry for 3–4 minutes until golden. Remove with a perforated spoon and drain. Keep hot while cooking the remaining mandazis. Dust with confectioner's sugar and serve at once.

HOT BANANAS WITH RUM AND RAISINS

Choose almost-ripe bananas with evenly colored skins, either all yellow or just green at the tips. Black patches indicate that the fruit is over-ripe.

Serves 4

¼ cup seedless raisins

5 tbsp dark rum

4 tbsp sweet butter

4 tbsp brown sugar

4 ripe bananas, peeled and
    halved lengthwise

¼ tsp grated nutmeg

¼ tsp ground cinnamon

2 tbsp slivered almonds, toasted

chilled cream or vanilla ice cream, to
    serve (optional)

Put the raisins in a bowl and pour over the rum. Leave to soak for about 30 minutes, by which time the raisins will have plumped up.

Melt the butter in a skillet, add the brown sugar, and stir until just dissolved. Add the bananas and cook them for 4–5 minutes until they are just tender.

Sprinkle the nutmeg and cinnamon over the bananas, then pour over the rum and raisins. Stand back and carefully set the rum alight, using a long taper, and stir gently to mix.

Scatter the slivered almonds over the bananas and serve immediately with chilled cream or vanilla ice cream, if you like. Crème fraîche or Greek-style yogurt would also make a delicious accompaniment for the bananas.

VARIATION

Try using golden raisins soaked in a tangerine-flavored liqueur, such as Van der Hum, or an orange-flavored liqueur, such as Grand Marnier, instead of raisins in rum.

BAKED APPLES WITH CARAMEL SAUCE

The creamy caramel sauce adds a touch of sophistication to this traditional dish.

Serves 6

3 Granny Smith apples, cored but
  not peeled
3 Red Delicious apples, cored but
  not peeled
¾ cup brown sugar, firmly packed
¾ cup water
½ teaspoon grated nutmeg
¼ teaspoon ground
  black pepper
¼ cup walnut pieces
¼ cup golden raisins
4 tablespoons butter or
  margarine, diced

For the caramel sauce
1 tablespoon butter or margarine
½ cup whipping cream

COOK'S TIP
*Use a mixture of firm red and
gold pears instead of the apples.
Cook for 10 minutes longer.*

Preheat the oven to 375°F. Lightly grease a baking pan. With a small knife, enlarge the core opening at the stem end of each apple to about 1 inch in diameter. Arrange the apples in the pan, stem end up.

In a small pan, combine the brown sugar, water, nutmeg, and pepper. Boil the mixture, stirring, for 6 minutes. Mix together the walnuts and golden raisins. Spoon some of the walnut mixture into each apple. Top with some diced butter or margarine. Spoon the sugar sauce over and around the apples. Bake, basting occasionally, until the apples are just tender, about 50 minutes. Put the apples in a serving dish, reserving the sauce in the baking dish. Keep the apples warm.

To make the caramel sauce, mix the butter or margarine, cream, and reserved sauce in a pan. Bring to a boil, stirring, and simmer for 2 minutes until thickened. Let the sauce cool slightly before serving.

CARAMELIZED APPLES

A sweet, sticky dessert which is very quickly made, and usually very quickly eaten!

Serves 4

1½ pounds eating apples

½ cup sweet butter

1 ounce fresh white bread crumbs

½ cup ground almonds

finely grated rind of 2 lemons

4 tablespoons corn syrup

4 tablespoons clotted cream,

  to serve

COOK'S TIP

The easiest and quickest way to make bread crumbs is to put slices of bread into a food processor or blender. Coarsely chop the bread for several seconds until crumbs form. Take care not to overchop.

Peel and core the apples. Carefully cut the apples into ½-inch thick rings. Heat a wok and add the butter. When the butter has melted, add the apple rings and stir-fry for 4 minutes until golden and tender. Remove from the wok, reserving the butter. Add the bread crumbs to the hot butter and stir-fry for 1 minute.

Stir in the ground almonds and lemon rind and stir-fry for 3 minutes more, stirring constantly. Sprinkle the bread crumb mix over the apples, then drizzle warmed corn syrup over the top. Serve with the cream.

CHOCOLATE CHIP BANANA PANCAKES

Serve these delicious banana pancakes as a dessert topped with cream and toasted almonds.

Makes 16

2 ripe bananas

scant 1 cup milk

2 eggs

1¼ cups self-rising flour

⅓ cup ground almonds

1 tbsp superfine sugar

pinch of salt

3 tbsp dark chocolate chips

butter, for frying

For the topping

⅔ cup heavy cream

1 tbsp confectioner's sugar

½ cup toasted slivered almonds

VARIATION

For banana and blueberry pancakes, replace the chocolate with 1 cup fresh blueberries. Hot pancakes are simply delicious when they are served with ice cream.

In a bowl, mash the bananas with a fork. Mix in half of the milk, then beat in the eggs. Sift in the flour and add the ground almonds, sugar, and salt. Mix lightly. Add the remaining milk and the chocolate chips to produce a thick batter.

Heat a knob of butter in a large non-stick skillet. Spoon the pancake mixture into heaps, allowing room for them to spread. When bubbles appear on top of the pancakes, turn them over, and cook briefly on the other side. Remove and keep hot.

Whip the cream lightly with the confectioner's sugar. Spoon onto the pancakes and top each with a few slivered almonds.

BANANA, MAPLE, AND LIME PANCAKES

Pancakes are a treat any day of the week, especially when they are filled with bananas and maple syrup.

Serves 4

1 cup all-purpose flour

1 egg white

1 cup milk

sunflower oil, for frying

strips of lime rind, to decorate

For the filling

4 bananas, sliced

3 tbsp maple syrup or
*   corn syrup*

2 tbsp fresh lime juice

COOK'S TIP

Pancakes freeze well. To store
for later use, stack and
interleave them with baking
parchment, overwrap with foil,
and freeze for up to 3 months.
Thaw thoroughly and reheat
before using.

Mix the flour, egg white, and milk in a bowl. Add 4 tbsp cold water and beat until smooth and bubbly. Chill until needed.

Heat a little oil in a non-stick skillet and swirl in enough batter just to coat the base. Cook until golden, then turn over, and cook the other side. Keep hot while making the remaining pancakes.

Make the filling. Place the bananas, syrup, and lime juice in a pan and simmer gently for 1 minute. Spoon into the pancakes and fold into fourths. Sprinkle with strips of lime rind to decorate.

LEMON CREPES

These thin, lacy French crêpes are wonderfully versatile. They are good served very simply with just lemon juice and sugar.

Makes about 12
1 cup flour
2 teaspoons superfine sugar (for sweet crêpes)
2 eggs
scant 1½ cups milk
about 2 tablespoons melted butter
lemon juice, to serve
sugar, to serve (optional)

CRÊPE-MAKING TIPS
● *The batter can be made in a blender or food processor. It must have time to stand before using to incorporate more air.*
● *Crêpe batter should be the consistency of whipping cream. If the batter doesn't flow smoothly to make a thin crêpe, add a little more more liquid.*
● *If the batter is lumpy, strain before using.*

To make the crêpe batter, mix together the flour, sugar (for sweet crêpes), eggs, and milk. Let stand at least 20 minutes. Heat an 8-inch crêpe pan over medium heat. The pan is ready for cooking when a few drops of water sprinkled on the surface jump and sizzle immediately. Grease the pan lightly with melted butter. Ladle or pour 3–4 tablespoons batter into the pan. Quickly tilt and rotate the pan so the batter spreads out to cover the bottom thinly and evenly; pour out any excess batter.

Cook until the crêpe is set and small holes have appeared, 30–45 seconds. If the cooking seems to be taking too long, increase the heat slightly. Lift the edge of the crêpe with a metal spatula; the base of the crêpe should be lightly brown. Shake the pan vigorously back and forth to loosen the crêpe completely, then turn or flip it over. Cook the other side for about 30 seconds. Serve sprinkled with lemon juice and sugar, if using.

APPLE SOUFFLE OMELET

Apples sautéed until they are slightly caramelized make a delicious seasonal filling for sweet omelets.

Serves 2

4 eggs, separated
2 tablespoons light cream
1 tablespoon superfine sugar
1 tablespoon butter
confectioner's sugar, for dredging

For the filling

2 tablespoons butter
2 tablespoons brown sugar
1 eating apple, peeled, cored
and sliced
3 tablespoons light cream

To make the filling, heat the butter and sugar in a frying pan and sauté the apple slices until just tender. Stir in the cream and keep warm.

Place the egg yolks in a bowl with the cream and sugar and beat well. Whisk the egg whites until stiff, then fold into the yolk mixture.

Melt the butter in a large heavy-based frying pan, pour in the soufflé mixture and spread evenly. Cook for 1 minute until golden underneath, then place under a hot broiler to brown the top.

Slide the omelet on to a plate, add the apple mixture, then fold over. Sift the confectioner's sugar over thickly, then mark in a criss-cross pattern with a hot metal skewer. Serve immediately.

STRAWBERRY AND APPLE TART

A dish for lovers – apples and strawberries in perfect harmony.

Serves 4–6

2 firm, tart cooking apples (about
  1 pound), peeled, cored and sliced
2 cups strawberries, halved
4 tablespoons sugar
1 tablespoon cornstarch

For the pastry

1¼ cups self-rising flour
⅔ cup oatmeal
4 tablespoons sunflower margarine

COOK'S TIP

It is best to prepare apples just before you use them. If you do prepare them ahead, place the cut pieces in a bowl of lemony cold water to prevent them from browning.

Preheat the oven to 400°F. For the pastry, mix the flour and oatmeal in a bowl and rub in the margarine evenly. Stir in cold water to bind and form into a ball. Knead lightly until smooth. On a lightly-floured surface, roll out the pastry and line a 9-inch loose-based tart pan. Trim the edges, prick the base, line the pastry with wax paper and fill with baking beans. Roll out the trimmings and stamp out heart shapes using a cookie cutter. Bake for 10 minutes, remove the paper and beans, and bake for 10–15 minutes or until golden brown. Bake the hearts until golden. Place the apples in a pan with the strawberries, sugar, and cornstarch. Cover and cook gently, stirring, until the fruit is just tender. Spoon into the pastry shell and serve decorated with the pastry hearts.

APPLE MERINGUE TART

Like pears, quinces substitute well in most apple recipes and are quick and delicious. If you ever find any quinces, this is the ideal tart to use them in.

Serves 6

1½ pounds eating apples
juice of ½ lemon
2 tablespoons butter
4 tablespoons raw sugar
cream or ice cream, to serve

For the pastry
½ cup flour
¾ cup whole-wheat flour
pinch of salt
½ cup superfine sugar
6 tablespoons butter
1 egg, separated, plus 1 egg white

To make the pastry, sift the flours into a bowl with the salt, adding in the wheat flakes from the sifter. Add 1 tablespoon of the superfine sugar and rub in the butter until the mixture forms soft crumbs.

Work in the egg yolk and, if necessary, 1–2 tablespoons cold water. Knead lightly and bring together into a ball. Chill, covered or wrapped, for between 10 and 20 minutes.

Preheat the oven to 375°F. Roll the chilled pastry out on a lightly floured surface to form a 9-inch round and use to line an 8-inch pie pan. Line with wax paper and fill with baking beans. Bake blind for 15 minutes, then remove the paper and beans and cook for 5–10 minutes more, until the pastry is crisp and golden.

Meanwhile, peel, core, and slice the apples, then toss in lemon juice. Melt the butter, add the raw sugar and fry the apple until golden and just tender. Arrange in the pastry shell.

Preheat the oven to 425°F. Whisk the egg white until it is stiff. Whisk in half the remaining superfine sugar, then carefully fold in the rest. Pipe the meringue over the apples. Bake for 6–7 minutes. Serve the tart hot or cold with cream or ice cream.

DUTCH APPLE TART

Sliced almonds give this tart a wonderful crunchiness.

Serves 4–6

6 eating apples, peeled, cored
   and grated
4 tablespoons brown sugar
¼ teaspoon vanilla extract
½ teaspoon ground cinnamon
scant ¼ cup raisins
¼ cup sliced almonds, toasted
1 tablespoon superfine sugar,
   for sprinkling
whipped cream, to serve

For the pastry
1½ cups flour
generous ½ cup butter, cubed
   and softened
6 tablespoons superfine sugar
pinch of salt

Preheat the oven to 350°F. Lightly butter an 8-inch round springform pan and dust with a little flour.

To make the pastry, place the flour in a bowl with the butter and sugar, then squeeze together to form a firm dough. Knead lightly and bring together into a ball. Chill, covered or wrapped, for 1 hour.

Roll two-thirds of the chilled pastry out on a lightly floured surface to form a 10-inch round. Use this to line the base and two-thirds up the sides of the prepared pan, pressing the pastry up the sides with your fingers. Trim away any excess pastry.

Mix together the apples, sugar, vanilla extract, cinnamon, raisins, and almonds in a bowl. Spoon into the lined pan and level the surface. Fold the pastry edge above the level of the apples down over the filling.

Roll out the remaining pastry and cut into eight ½-inch strips. Brush the strips with cold water and sprinkle over the superfine sugar. Lay the strips on top of the tart in a lattice pattern, securing the ends to the folded-over edge with water.

Bake in the center of the oven for 1 hour, or until the pastry is golden brown. Remove and let cool in the pan. When the tart is cold, carefully remove it from the pan. Serve cut into slices with whipped cream.

RED BERRY SPONGE TART

Use a selection of berries for this delicious sponge tart. Serve warm from the oven with vanilla ice cream.

Serves 4

softened butter, for greasing

3 cups soft berry fruits, such as
*   raspberries, blackberries, black*
*   currants, red currants, strawberries*
*   or blueberries*

2 eggs, at room temperature

¼ cup superfine sugar, plus extra to
*   taste (optional)*

1 tablespoon flour

¾ cup ground almonds

vanilla ice cream, to serve

Preheat the oven to 375°F. Brush the base and sides of a 9-inch pie pan with softened butter and line the base with a circle of nonstick baking paper. Scatter the fruit in the pan with a little sugar if the fruits are tart.

Whisk the eggs and sugar together for about 3–4 minutes or until they leave a thick trail across the surface. Combine the flour and almonds, then fold into the egg mixture with a spatula – retaining as much air as possible.

Spread the mixture on top of the fruit base and bake in the oven for 15 minutes. Transfer to a serving plate and serve with vanilla ice cream.

LEMON ALMOND TART

This classic tart is fresh-tasting, with a crisp, sweet pastry shell.

Serves 8

8 ounces short pastry dough

3/4 cup blanched almonds

1/2 cup sugar

2 eggs

grated rind and juice of 1 1/2 lemons

1/2 cup (1 stick) butter, melted

strips of lemon rind, to decorate

Roll out the dough to about 1/8 inch thick and transfer to a 9-inch tart pan. Trim the edge. Prick the base all over and chill for at least 20 minutes.

Preheat the oven to 400°F. Line the tart shell with crumpled wax paper and fill with pie weights. Bake for 12 minutes. Remove the paper and weights and continue baking until golden, 6–8 minutes more. Reduce the oven temperature to 350°F. Grind the almonds finely with 1 tablespoon of the sugar in a food processor, blender, or nut grinder. Set a mixing bowl over a pan of hot water. Add the eggs and the remaining sugar, and beat with an electric mixer until the mixture is very thick. Stir in the lemon rind and juice, butter, and ground almonds.

Pour into the pastry shell. Bake until the filling is golden and set, about 35 minutes. Decorate with lemon rind.

RED BERRY TART WITH LEMON CREAM FILLING

Just right for warm summer days, this tart is best filled just before serving so the pastry remains mouth-wateringly crisp. Select a range of berries such as strawberries, raspberries or red currants.

Serves 6–8

1¼ cups flour
¼ cup cornstarch
3 tablespoons confectioner's sugar
8 tablespoons butter
1 teaspoon vanilla extract
2 egg yolks, beaten

For the filling

1 cup cream cheese, softened
3 tablespoons lemon cheese
grated rind and juice of 1 lemon
confectioner's sugar, to sweeten
  (optional)
1½ cups mixed red berry fruits
3 tablespoons red currant jelly

Sift the flour, cornstarch and confectioner's sugar together, then rub in the butter until the mixture resembles bread crumbs.

Beat the vanilla into the egg yolks, then mix into the crumbs to make a firm dough, adding cold water if necessary.

Roll out and line a 9-inch round pie pan, pressing the dough well up the sides after trimming. Prick the base of the tart with a fork and allow it to rest in the fridge for 30 minutes.

Preheat the oven to 400°F. Line the tart with waxed paper and baking beans. Place the pan on a cookie sheet and bake for 20 minutes, removing the paper and beans for the last 5 minutes. When cooked, cool and remove the pastry shell from the pie pan.

Cream the cheese, lemon cheese and lemon rind and juice, adding a little confectioner's sugar to sweeten, if you wish. Spread the mixture into the tart.

Top the tart with the fruits. Warm the red currant jelly and trickle it over the fruits just before serving.

VARIATION
Leave out the red currant jelly, if you prefer.

TARTE TATIN

This delicious caramelized fruit tart from France was originally created by the Tatin sisters who ran a popular restaurant in Sologne in the Orléanais.

Serves 4

6 tablespoons butter, softened

6 tablespoons brown sugar, firmly packed

10 firm, sweet eating apples, peeled, cored and thickly sliced

whipped cream, to serve (optional)

For the pastry

4 tablespoons butter, softened

3 tablespoons superfine sugar

1 egg

1 cup flour

pinch of salt

COOK'S TIP

It is important to use firm apples for this tart so that they will hold their shape well during cooking. Any type of firm eating apples will be suitable.

To make the pastry, cream the butter and sugar in a bowl until pale and creamy. Beat in the egg, then sift in the flour and salt and mix to a soft dough. On a lightly floured surface, knead gently and bring together into a ball. Chill, covered or wrapped, for 1 hour.

Grease a 9-inch cake pan, then add 4 tablespoons of the butter. Place the cake pan on the burner and melt the butter gently. Remove and sprinkle over 4 tablespoons of the sugar.

Arrange the apple slices on top, then sprinkle with the remaining sugar and dot with the remaining butter.

Preheat the oven to 450°F. Place the cake pan on the burner again over a low to moderate heat for about 15 minutes, until a light golden caramel forms on the base. Remove the pan from the heat.

Roll out the pastry on a lightly floured surface to a round the same size as the pan and lay on top of the apples. Tuck the pastry edges down around the sides of the apples. Trim away any excess pastry.

Bake for about 20–25 minutes, until the pastry is golden brown. Remove the tart from the oven and let stand for about 5 minutes.

Place an upturned plate on top of the pan and, holding the two together with a dish towel, turn the apple tart out on to the plate. Serve while still warm with whipped cream, if wished.

STRAWBERRY AND BLUEBERRY TART

This tart works equally well using any combination of berries – as long as there is a riot of color and the fruit is in perfect condition.

Serves 6–8

2 cups flour

pinch of salt

9 tablespoons confectioner's sugar

10 tablespoons sweet butter, diced

1 egg yolk

For the filling

1¼ cups mascarpone

2 tablespoons confectioner's sugar

few drops vanilla extract

finely grated rind of 1 orange

3–5 cups fresh mixed strawberries
* and blueberries*

6 tablespoons red currant jelly

2 tablespoons orange juice

Sift the flour, salt and sugar into a bowl, and rub in the butter until the mixture resembles coarse crumbs. Using a round-bladed knife, mix in the egg yolk and 2 teaspoons cold water. Gather the dough together, then turn out on to a floured surface and knead lightly until smooth. Wrap in plastic wrap and chill for 1 hour.

Preheat the oven to 375°F. Roll out the pastry and use to line a 10-inch fluted quiche pan. Prick the base and chill for 15 minutes.

Line the chilled pastry shell with wax paper and baking beans, then bake for 15 minutes. Remove the paper and beans and bake for a further 15 minutes, until crisp and golden. Leave to cool in the pan.

Beat together the mascarpone, sugar, vanilla extract and orange rind in a mixing bowl until the mixture is smooth.

Remove the pastry shell from the pan, then spoon in the filling and pile the fruits on top. Heat the red currant jelly with the orange juice until runny, strain if necessary, then brush over the fruit to glaze.

APPLE PIE

A comforting dish that will take you back to your childhood.

Serves 8

*4 firm, tart cooking apples (about
  2 pounds), sliced*

1 tablespoon fresh lemon juice

1 teaspoon vanilla extract

½ cup sugar

½ teaspoon ground cinnamon

1½ tablespoons butter or margarine

1 egg yolk

2 teaspoons whipping cream

For the pastry

2 cups flour

1 teaspoon salt

¾ cup shortening

4–5 tablespoons ice water

1 tablespoon quick-cooking tapioca

Preheat the oven to 450°F. To make the pastry, sift the flour and salt into a bowl. Rub in the shortening until the mixture forms soft crumbs. Add the water, a tablespoon at a time, and bring together into a ball.

Cut the dough in half and shape each half into another ball. On a lightly floured surface, roll out one of the balls to a circle about 12 inches in diameter.

Line a lightly greased 9-inch pie pan, easing the dough in and being careful not to stretch it. Trim the edges carefully and keep the excess pastry for later. Sprinkle the tapioca evenly over the base of the pastry shell.

Roll out the remaining pastry to ⅛ inch thick and cut out eight large leaf shapes with a sharp knife. Cut the trimmings into enough smaller leaves to decorate the edges of the pie. Score the leaves with the back of a knife to make the leaf veins.

To make the filling, mix together the apples, lemon juice, vanilla extract, sugar, and cinnamon. Tip into the pastry shell and add dots of butter or margarine over the apple mixture.

Arrange the large pastry leaves in a decorative pattern on top, and decorate the edges with the smaller leaves. Mix the egg yolk with the cream and brush it over the leaves.

Bake in the preheated oven for 10 minutes. Reduce the oven temperature to 350°F. Cook for 35–45 minutes more until the pastry is golden brown. Allow the pie to cool in the pan slightly before removing it and putting it on a wire cooling rack.

BLUEBERRY AND PEAR PIE

The combination of blueberries and pears makes a sweet and juicy pie. Serve warm with cream, or try a scoop or two of vanilla ice cream.

Serves 4

2 cups flour

pinch of salt

4 tablespoons shortening

4 tablespoons butter, cubed

6 cups blueberries

2 tablespoons superfine sugar

1 tablespoon arrowroot

2 ripe, but firm pears, peeled, cored and sliced

1/2 teaspoon ground cinnamon

grated rind of 1/2 lemon

beaten egg, to glaze

sugar, for sprinkling

crème fraîche or heavy cream, to serve

Sift the flour and salt into a bowl and rub in the shortening and butter until the mixture resembles fine bread crumbs. Stir in 3 tablespoons cold water and mix to a dough. Chill for 30 minutes.

Place 2 cups of the blueberries in a pan with the sugar. Cover and cook gently until the blueberries have softened. Press through a nylon strainer.

Blend the arrowroot with 2 tablespoons cold water and add to the blueberry purée. Bring to a boil, stirring until thickened. Cool slightly.

Place a cookie sheet in the oven and preheat to 375°F. Roll out just over half the pastry on a lightly floured surface and use to line an 8-inch shallow pie pan.

Mix together the remaining blueberries, the pears, cinnamon and lemon rind and spoon into the dish. Pour the blueberry purée over.

Roll out the remaining pastry and use to cover the pie. Make a small slit in the center. Brush with beaten egg and sprinkle with sugar. Bake the pie on the hot cookie sheet, for 40–45 minutes, until golden. Serve warm with crème fraîche or heavy cream.

APPLE AND PEAR SKILLET CAKE

This unusual cake, lightly spiced with cinnamon and nutmeg and baked in a frying pan, is impressively simple to make. It is delicious served hot.

Serves 6

1 apple, peeled, cored and thinly sliced

1 pear, peeled, cored and thinly sliced

½ cup walnut pieces, chopped

1 teaspoon ground cinnamon

1 teaspoon grated nutmeg

3 eggs

¾ cup flour

2 tablespoons brown sugar,
*   firmly packed*

¾ cup milk

1 teaspoon vanilla extract

4 tablespoons butter or margarine

confectioner's sugar, for sprinkling

cream or ice cream, to serve (optional)

Preheat the oven to 375°F. In a large bowl, toss together the apple slices, pear slices, walnuts, cinnamon, and nutmeg until thoroughly combined. Set aside.

With an electric mixer, beat together the eggs, flour, brown sugar, milk, and vanilla extract. Melt the butter or margarine in a 9- or 10-inch ovenproof frying pan (preferably cast-iron) over moderate heat. Add the apple mixture and cook for about 5 minutes, until it is lightly caramelized, stirring occasionally. When cooked, make sure that the apple and pear mixture is evenly distributed in the frying pan.

Pour the sponge mixture over the fruit and nuts. Transfer the skillet to the preheated oven and bake for about 30 minutes, until the cake is puffy and pulls away from the sides of the pan. Serve hot sprinkled with confectioner's sugar, with cream or ice cream as an accompaniment, if you wish.

COOK'S TIP

This cake should be served straight from the frying pan. There is no need to transfer it to a serving plate first.

APPLE AND BLACKBERRY NUT CRUMBLE

This much-loved dish is perhaps one of the simplest and most delicious of traditional hot desserts.

Serves 4

*4 firm, tart cooking apples (about
  2 pounds), peeled, cored and sliced*
½ cup butter, cubed
⅝ cup brown sugar, firmly packed
1¾ cups blackberries

For the topping
¾ cup whole wheat flour
¾ cup flour
½ teaspoon ground cinnamon
*3 tablespoons chopped mixed
  nuts, toasted*
custard, cream, or ice cream, to serve

Preheat the oven to 350°F. Lightly butter a 5-cup ovenproof dish. Place the apples in a pan with 2 tablespoons of the butter, 2 tablespoons of the sugar, and 1 tablespoon water. Cover and cook gently for about 10 minutes, until just tender. Remove from the heat and gently stir in the blackberries. Spoon the mixture into the dish and set aside.

To make the crumble topping, sift the flours and cinnamon into a bowl (tip in any of the wheat flakes left in the sifter). Add the remaining 6 tablespoons butter and rub into the flour with your fingertips until the mixture resembles fine crumbs (or you can use a food processor or blender).

Stir in the remaining 6 tablespoons sugar and the nuts and mix well. Sprinkle the crumble topping over the fruit. Bake for 35–40 minutes, until the top is golden brown. Serve hot with custard, cream, or ice cream.

APPLE COUSCOUS PUDDING

This unusual couscous mixture makes a delicious dessert with a rich, fruity flavor, but virtually no fat.

Serves 4

2½ cups apple juice

⅔ cup couscous

¼ cup raisins

½ teaspoon mixed spice

1 large tart, firm cooking apple, peeled, cored and sliced

2 tablespoons raw sugar

plain low-fat yogurt, to serve

Preheat the oven to 400°F. Place the apple juice, couscous, raisins, and spice in a pan and bring to a boil, stirring. Cover and simmer for 10–12 minutes, until all the free liquid is absorbed.

Spoon half the couscous mixture into a 5-cup ovenproof dish and top with half the apple slices. Top with the remaining couscous.

Arrange the remaining apple slices overlapping over the top and sprinkle with raw sugar. Bake in the oven for 25–30 minutes, or until golden brown. Serve hot with yogurt.

COOK'S TIP

To ring the changes, substitute other dried fruits for the raisins in this recipe – try chopped dates or ready-to-eat pears, figs, peaches, or apricots.

APPLE AND KUMQUAT SPONGE PUDDINGS

The kumquats provide a surprising tanginess in this dessert.

Serves 8

generous ½ cup butter, at room
  temperature
6 ounces firm, tart cooking apples,
  peeled and thinly sliced
3 ounces kumquats, thinly sliced
generous ½ cup superfine sugar
2 eggs
1 cup self-rising flour

For the sauce

3 ounces kumquats, thinly sliced
6 tablespoons superfine sugar
1 cup water
⅔ cup crème fraîche
1 teaspoon cornstarch mixed with
  2 teaspoons water
lemon juice, to taste

Prepare the steamer. Lightly butter eight ⅔-cup dariole molds or rame-kins and put a disc of buttered waxed paper on the base of each one.

Melt 2 tablespoons butter in a frying pan. Add the apples, kumquats, and 2 tablespoons sugar and cook over a moderate heat for 5–8 minutes or until the apples start to soften and the sugar begins to caramelize. Remove from the heat and let cool.

Meanwhile, cream the remaining butter with the remaining sugar until the mixture is pale and fluffy. Add the eggs, one at a time, beating well after each addition. Fold in the flour.

Divide the apple and kumquat mixture among the prepared molds. Top with the sponge mixture. Cover the molds and put them into the steamer. Steam on top of the burner for 45 minutes.

To make the sauce, put the kumquats, sugar, and water in a frying pan and bring to a boil, stirring to dissolve the sugar. Simmer for 5 minutes. Stir in the crème fraîche and bring back to a boil, stirring.

Remove from the heat and whisk in the cornstarch mixture. Return the pan to the heat and simmer gently for 2 minutes more, stirring constantly. Add lemon juice to taste. Turn out the puddings and serve hot with the kumquat sauce.

cakes and tea breads

Everyone is familiar with the use of dried fruit in cakes
and tea breads, but the following recipes show what
fabulous results can be achieved with fresh fruit.
Some of the cakes and breads may be enjoyed either
warm from the oven or at room temperature.
Try Apple Crumble Cake, Orange Honey Bread,
Warm Lemon and Syrup Cake and the luscious
Chocolate Cake with Banana Sauce.

LEMON COCONUT LAYER CAKE

This delightful layered cake has a tangy lemon custard sauce filling and a light lemony frosting, contrasting with the crunchy coconut topping.

Serves 8–10

1 cup flour

pinch of salt

8 eggs

1¾ cups sugar

1 tablespoon grated orange rind

grated rind of 2 lemons

juice of 1 lemon

½ cup shredded coconut

2 tablespoons cornstarch

1 cup water

6 tablespoons butter

For the frosting

½ cup (1 stick) sweet butter, at room
*   temperature*

1 cup confectioner's sugar

grated rind of 1 lemon

6 tablespoons fresh lemon juice, plus
*   more if needed*

14-ounce can shredded coconut

Preheat the oven to 350°F. Line three 8-inch cake pans with wax paper and grease. In a bowl, sift together the flour and salt and set aside.

Place six of the eggs in a large heatproof bowl set over hot water. With an electric mixer, beat until frothy. Gradually beat in ¾ cup of the sugar until the mixture doubles in volume, about 10 minutes.

Remove the bowl from the hot water. Fold in the orange rind and half of the grated lemon rind. Gently stir in 1 tablespoon of the lemon juice. Fold in the coconut. Sift over the flour mixture in three batches, folding in after each addition. Divide the mixture between the prepared pans.

Bake until the cakes pull away from the sides of the pan, 25–30 minutes. Let stand 3–5 minutes, then unmold and transfer to a wire rack.

In a bowl, blend the cornstarch with a little cold water to dissolve. Whisk in the remaining eggs just until blended. Set aside.

In a saucepan, combine the remaining lemon rind and juice, the water, remaining sugar, and butter. Over moderate heat, bring the mixture to a boil. Whisk in the eggs and cornstarch, and return to a boil. Whisk continuously until thick, about 5 minutes. Remove from the heat. Cover with wax paper to stop a skin forming and set aside. For the frosting, cream the butter and confectioner's sugar until smooth. Stir in the lemon rind and enough lemon juice to obtain a thick, spreadable consistency.

Sandwich the three cake layers with the lemon custard sauce mixture. Spread the frosting over the top and sides. Cover the cake all over with the shredded coconut, pressing it in gently.

BANANA AND LEMON CAKE

Light, moist, and flavorsome, this cake keeps very well and is everybody's favorite.

Serves 8–10

2¼ cups all-purpose flour

1¼ tsp baking powder

pinch of salt

½ cup sweet butter, at room
   temperature

scant 1 cup superfine sugar

½ cup brown sugar

2 eggs

½ tsp grated lemon rind

1 cup mashed, very
   ripe bananas

1 tsp vanilla extract

4 tbsp milk

¾ cup chopped walnuts

lemon-rind curls, to decorate

For the frosting

½ cup butter, at room
   temperature

4½ cups confectioner's sugar

1 tsp grated lemon rind

3–5 tbsp lemon juice

Preheat the oven to 350°F. Grease two 9in round cake pans, and line the bases with baking parchment. Sift the flour, baking powder, and salt into a bowl.

Beat the butter and sugars in a large mixing bowl, until light and fluffy. Beat in the eggs, one at a time, then stir in the grated lemon rind.

Mix the mashed bananas with the vanilla extract and milk in a small bowl. Stir this, in batches, into the creamed butter mixture, alternating with the sifted flour. Stir lightly until just blended. Fold in the walnuts.

Divide the mixture between the cake pans and spread evenly. Bake for 30–35 minutes, until a skewer inserted in the center comes out clean. Leave to stand for 5 minutes before turning out onto a wire rack. Peel off the lining parchment and leave to cool.

Make the frosting. Cream the butter in a bowl until smooth, then gradually beat in the confectioner's sugar. Stir in the lemon rind and enough of the lemon juice to make a spreading consistency.

Place one of the cakes on a serving plate. Spread over one-third of the frosting, then top with the second cake. Spread the remaining frosting evenly over the top and sides of the cake. Decorate with lemon-rind curls.

SUMMER STRAWBERRY GATEAU

No one could resist the appeal of little heartsease pansies. This strawberry-filled cake would be lovely for a summer occasion in the garden.

Serves 6–8

scant ½ cup soft margarine

scant ½ cup sugar

2 teaspoons clear honey

1¼ cups self-rising flour

½ teaspoon baking powder

2 tablespoons milk

2 eggs, plus 1 egg white for crystallizing

1 tablespoon rose water

1 tablespoon Cointreau or
* orange liqueur*

16 heartsease pansy flowers

superfine sugar, to crystallize

confectioner's sugar, to decorate

3 cups strawberries

strawberry leaves, to decorate

Preheat the oven to 375°F. Grease and lightly flour a ring mold. Put the soft margarine, sugar, honey, flour, baking powder, milk and 2 eggs into a mixing bowl and beat well for 1 minute. Add the rose water and Cointreau or orange liqueur and mix well.

Pour the mixture into the prepared pan and bake for 40 minutes or until a skewer inserted in the center comes out clean. Allow to stand for a few minutes and then turn out on to the plate that you wish to serve it on and leave to cool.

Crystallize the heartsease pansies by first painting them with lightly beaten egg white and then sprinkling with superfine sugar. Leave them to dry completely.

Sift a little confectioner's sugar over the cake. Fill the center of the ring with strawberries and decorate with the crystallized pansies and some strawberry leaves.

BERRY SHORTCAKE

This classic dessert can be assembled up to an hour ahead and kept chilled until required.

Serves 8

1¼ cups whipping cream

*2 tablespoons confectioner's
sugar, sifted*

*4 cups berries (strawberries or mixed
berries), halved or sliced if large*

¼ cup sugar, or to taste

For the shortcake biscuit

2 cups flour

2 teaspoons baking powder

5 tablespoons superfine sugar

½ cup butter

5 tablespoons milk

1 extra-large egg

Preheat the oven to 450°F. Grease an 8-inch round cake pan. To make the shortcake biscuit, sift the flour, baking powder, and sugar into a bowl. Add the butter and cut or rub in until the mixture resembles fine crumbs. Combine the milk and egg. Add to the crumb mixture and stir just until evenly mixed to a soft dough.

Put the dough in the prepared pan and pat out to an even layer. Bake until a wooden skewer inserted in the center comes out clean, 15–20 minutes. Let cool slightly.

Whip the cream until it starts to thicken. Add the confectioner's sugar and continue whipping until the cream will hold soft peaks.

Put the berries in a bowl. Sprinkle with the sugar and toss together lightly. Cover and set aside for the berries to render some juice.

Remove the shortcake biscuit from the pan. With a long, serrated knife, split it horizontally into two equal layers.

Put the bottom layer on a serving plate. Top with half of the berries and most of the cream. Set the second layer on top and press down gently. Spoon the remaining berries over the top layer (or serve them separately) and add the remaining cream in small, decorative dollops.

CRANBERRY AND APPLE RING

Tangy cranberries add an unusual flavor to this light-textured cake. It is best eaten very fresh.

Serves 4–6

2 cups self-rising flour

1 teaspoon ground cinnamon

6 tablespoons brown sugar

1 crisp eating apple, cored and diced

2/3 cup fresh or frozen cranberries

4 tablespoons sunflower oil

2/3 cup apple juice

cranberry jelly and apple slices,
*   to decorate*

Preheat the oven to 350°F. Lightly grease a 4-cup ring pan with oil. It is easiest to do this with a pastry brush, or you could use a paper towel.

Sift together the flour and ground cinnamon, then stir in the sugar. Toss together the diced apple and cranberries. Stir the fruit into the dry ingredients, then add the sunflower oil and apple juice and beat well until thoroughly combined.

Spoon the cake mixture into the prepared ring pan and bake in the preheated oven for about 35–40 minutes, or until the cake is firm to the touch. Turn the cake out and let cool completely on a wire cooling rack.

Just before serving, warm the cranberry jelly in a small saucepan over gentle heat. Decorate the top of the ring with the prepared apple slices, then drizzle the warmed cranberry jelly over the apple pieces, letting it run down the sides of the ring.

COOK'S TIP

Fresh cranberries are readily available throughout the winter months and if you don't use them all at once, they can be frozen for up to a year.

APPLE CRUMBLE CAKE

A rich and filling cake which is excellent served with thick cream or custard.

Serves 8–10

For the topping

¾ cup self-rising flour

½ teaspoon ground cinnamon

3 tablespoons butter

2 tablespoons sugar

For the base

4 tablespoons butter, softened

6 tablespoons sugar

1 large egg, beaten

1 cup self-rising flour, sifted

*2 firm, tart cooking apples (about
    1 pound), peeled, cored and sliced*

⅓ cup golden raisins

To decorate

*1 red eating apple, cored, thinly sliced
    and tossed in lemon juice*

2 tablespoons superfine sugar, sifted

pinch of ground cinnamon

Preheat the oven to 350°F. Lightly grease and line a deep 7-inch springform pan.

To make the topping, sift the flour and cinnamon together into a bowl. Rub in the butter until the mixture forms soft crumbs, then stir in the sugar. Set aside until needed.

To make the base for the cake, put the butter, sugar, egg, and flour into a bowl and beat for 1–2 minutes until smooth. Spoon into the prepared pan and even out the surface.

Mix together the apple slices and golden raisins and spread them evenly over the top of the base. Sprinkle with the topping.

Bake in the center of the preheated oven for about 1 hour. Then remove from the oven and cool in the pan for 10 minutes before turning out on to a wire cooling rack and peeling off the lining paper. Serve warm or cool, decorated with the prepared slices of red eating apple, and with sugar and cinnamon sprinkled over the top.

WARM LEMON AND SYRUP CAKE

After soaking in a tangy lemon syrup, this cake is both delightfully sweet and tart.

Serves 8

3 eggs

¾ cup butter, softened

¾ cup superfine sugar

1½ cups self-rising flour

½ cup ground almonds

¼ teaspoon ground nutmeg

*2 ounces candied lemon peel, finely
  chopped*

grated rind of 1 lemon

2 tablespoons lemon juice

poached pears, to serve

For the syrup

¾ cup superfine sugar

juice of 3 lemons

Preheat the oven to 350°F. Grease and line the base of a deep, round 8-inch cake pan.

Place all the cake ingredients in a large bowl and beat together for 2–3 minutes, until light and fluffy.

Tip the mixture into the prepared pan, spread level and bake for 1 hour, or until golden and firm to the touch.

Meanwhile, make the syrup. Put the sugar, lemon juice and 5 tablespoons water in a pan. Heat gently, stirring until the sugar has dissolved, then boil, without stirring, for 1–2 minutes.

Turn out the cake on to a plate with a rim. Prick the surface of the cake all over with a fork, then pour over the hot syrup. Leave to soak for about 30 minutes. Serve the cake warm with thin wedges of poached pears.

CHOCOLATE CAKE WITH BANANA SAUCE

Caramelized banana and rum sauce tastes superb with wedges of chocolate cake.

Serves 6

4oz dark chocolate, broken into
*   squares*
½ cup sweet butter, at room
*   temperature*
1 tbsp instant coffee powder
5 eggs, separated
1 cup sugar
1 cup all-purpose flour
1 tsp ground cinnamon

For the sauce

4 ripe bananas
4 tbsp brown sugar
1 tbsp lemon juice
¾ cup heavy cream
1 tbsp rum (optional)

Preheat the oven to 350°F. Grease an 8in round cake pan. Bring a small saucepan of water to a boil. Remove it from the heat and place a heatproof bowl on top. Add the chocolate and butter to the bowl and leave until melted, stirring occasionally. Stir in the coffee powder and set aside.

Mix the egg yolks and sugar in a bowl. Beat by hand or with an electric mixer until thick and lemon-colored. Add the chocolate mixture and beat on low speed for just long enough to blend the mixtures evenly.

Sift the flour and cinnamon into a bowl. In another bowl, whisk the egg whites to stiff peaks. Fold a spoon of egg white into the chocolate mixture to lighten it. Fold in the remaining egg white in batches, alternating with the sifted flour mixture.

Pour the mixture into the prepared pan. Bake for 40–50 minutes or until a skewer inserted in the center comes out clean. Turn out onto a wire rack.

Preheat the broiler. Make the sauce. Slice the bananas into a shallow, flameproof dish. Add the brown sugar and lemon juice and stir to mix. Place under the broiler and cook, stirring occasionally, for about 8 minutes until the sugar is caramelized and bubbling. Mash the bananas into the sauce until almost smooth. Stir in the cream and rum, if using. Slice the cake and serve it warm, with the sauce.

PINEAPPLE AND GINGER CAKE

This tasty cake is packed with flavors; apricot and pineapple are combined with tangy orange and lemon, and spiked with the refreshing, peppery taste of ginger.

Serves 10–12

3/4 cup sweet butter

3/4 cup superfine sugar

3 eggs, beaten

few drops of vanilla extract

2 cups flour, sifted

1/4 teaspoon salt

1 1/2 teaspoons baking powder

1 1/3 cups ready-to-eat dried apricots, chopped

1/2 cup each chopped crystallized ginger and crystallized pineapple

grated rind and juice of 1/2 orange

grated rind and juice of 1/2 lemon

a little milk

Preheat the oven to 350°F. Double line an 8-inch round or 7-inch square cake pan. Cream the butter and sugar together until light and fluffy.

Gradually beat the eggs into the creamed mixture with the vanilla extract, beating well after each addition. Sift together the flour, salt and baking powder into a bowl, and add a little to the mixture with the last of the egg, then fold in the rest.

Fold in the fruit, ginger and fruit rinds gently, then add sufficient fruit juice and milk to give a fairly soft dropping consistency.

Spoon the mixture into the prepared pan and smooth the top with a wet spoon. Bake for 20 minutes, then reduce the oven temperature to 325°F for a further 1 1/2–2 hours, or until firm to the touch and a skewer comes out of the center clean.

Leave the cake to cool in the pan completely, then turn out and wrap in fresh paper before storing in an airtight tin.

COOK'S TIP
This is not a long-keeping cake, but it does freeze, well-wrapped in waxed paper and then overwrapped in foil.

BANANA NUT BREAD

Banana bread is always popular. This delicious, healthy version has added pecans.

Makes 1 loaf

½ cup sweet butter, at room
*   temperature*
½ cup sugar
2 eggs, at room temperature
1 cup all-purpose flour
1 tsp baking soda
¼ tsp salt
1 tsp ground cinnamon
½ cup whole wheat flour
3 large ripe bananas
1 tsp vanilla extract
½ cup pecan nuts, chopped

COOK'S TIP

If the cake mixture shows signs
of curdling when you add the
eggs, beat in a little of the sifted
flour mixture.

Preheat the oven to 350°F. Line the bottom and sides of a 9 x 5in loaf pan with baking parchment.

Using an electric mixer, cream the butter and sugar in a bowl until light and fluffy. Add the eggs, one at a time, beating well after each addition.

Sift the all-purpose flour, baking soda, salt, and cinnamon over the butter mixture. Stir in thoroughly, then stir in the whole wheat flour.

Mash the bananas to a purée, then stir into the mixture. Stir in the vanilla extract and pecans. Pour into the prepared pan and level the surface.

Bake the loaf for 50–60 minutes, until a skewer inserted in the center comes out clean. Turn out onto a wire rack to cool.

ORANGE HONEY BREAD

Honey improves the keeping quality of cakes and breads, but this is so delicious that you are unlikely to be able to put the theory to the test.

Makes 1 loaf

2½ cups flour

2½ teaspoons baking powder

½ teaspoon baking soda

½ teaspoon salt

2 tablespoons margarine

1 cup clear honey

1 egg, lightly beaten

¼ cup grated orange rind

¾ cup fresh
   orange juice

¾ cup chopped walnuts

Preheat the oven to 325°F. Grease a 9 x 5-inch loaf pan and line the base with non-stick baking paper. Sift the flour, baking powder, baking soda and salt together.

Cream the margarine in a mixing bowl until soft. Stir in the honey until well mixed, then stir in the lightly beaten egg. Add the orange rind and stir to combine thoroughly.

Fold the flour mixture into the honey and egg mixture in three batches, alternating with the orange juice. Stir in the walnuts.

Pour into the prepared pan and bake for about 1 hour or until a cake tester inserted in the center of the loaf comes out clean. Let stand for 10 minutes before turning out onto a wire rack to cool.

BANANA GINGER CAKE

Bananas and ginger make a winning combination. This cake actually improves with keeping.

Makes 12 bars

1¾ cups all-purpose flour

2 tsp baking soda

2 tsp ground ginger

1¾ cups medium oatmeal

4 tbsp dark brown sugar

6 tbsp butter or margarine

⅔ cup corn syrup

1 egg, beaten

3 ripe bananas, mashed

¾ cup confectioner's sugar

preserved ginger, to decorate

COOK'S TIP

This is a nutritious, energy-giving cake that is a good choice for brown-bag lunches, as it doesn't break up or crumble very easily.

Preheat the oven to 325°F. Grease and line an 11 x 7in cake pan with baking parchment. Sift the flour, baking soda, and ground ginger into a bowl, then stir in the oatmeal.

Melt the sugar, butter or margarine, and syrup in a saucepan, then stir into the flour mixture. Beat in the egg and mashed bananas.

Spoon the mixture into the pan and bake for about 1 hour, or until firm to the touch. Allow to cool in the pan, then turn out, and cut into bars.

Sift the confectioner's sugar into a bowl and stir in just enough water to make a smooth, runny frosting. Drizzle the frosting over each square and top with slices of preserved ginger.

BANANA MUFFINS

Make plenty of these delectable treats – banana muffins are irresistible at any time of the day.

Makes 10

2 cups all-purpose flour

1 tsp baking powder

1 tsp baking soda

¼ tsp salt

¼ tsp grated nutmeg

½ tsp ground cinnamon

3 large ripe bananas

1 egg

⅓ cup brown sugar

4 tbsp vegetable oil

¼ cup raisins

Preheat the oven to 375°F. Line 10 muffin cups with paper liners or grease them lightly. Sift the flour, baking powder, baking soda, salt, nutmeg, and cinnamon into a bowl. Set aside.

Mash the bananas in a mixing bowl until creamy. Using a hand-held electric mixer, beat in the egg, sugar, and oil. Add the dry ingredients and mix until just blended. Stir in the raisins.

Fill the muffin cups two-thirds full. Bake for 20–25 minutes or until the tops spring back when lightly touched. Transfer the muffins to a wire rack to cool slightly. Serve warm.

COOK'S TIP

If there are any empty cups in the muffin tray when you have used up the mixture, fill them with water before placing the tray in the oven to ensure that the muffins bake evenly.

CHOCOLATE AND BANANA BROWNIES

Bananas give brownies a delicious flavor and keep them marvelously moist.

Makes 9

5 tbsp cocoa powder

1 tbsp superfine sugar

5 tbsp milk

3 large bananas, mashed

1 cup brown sugar

1 tsp vanilla extract

5 egg whites

¾ cup self-rising flour

⅔ cup oat bran

1 tbsp confectioner's sugar, for
    dusting

COOK'S TIP

Store these brownies in an airtight container for one day before eating them – their flavor becomes stronger and improves with keeping.

Preheat the oven to 350°F. Line an 8in square baking pan with baking parchment. In a bowl, mix the cocoa powder and superfine sugar with the milk. Add the bananas, brown sugar, and vanilla extract. Mix well.

In a mixing bowl, beat the egg whites lightly with a fork. Add the chocolate mixture and continue to beat well. Sift the flour over the mixture and fold in with the oat bran. Pour into the prepared pan.

Bake for 40 minutes or until firm. Cool in the pan for 10 minutes, then turn out onto a wire rack, and cool completely. Cut into nine wedges and dust lightly with confectioner's sugar before serving.

LEMON SPICE COOKIES

These crisp cookies are perfect for most occasions and are delicious served with ice cream.

Makes 50

2⅛ *cups flour*

½ *teaspoon salt*

2 *teaspoons ground cinnamon*

1 *cup (2 sticks) sweet butter, at room*
   temperature

1 *cup sugar*

2 *eggs*

1 *teaspoon vanilla extract*

grated rind of 1 lemon

In a bowl, sift together the flour, salt, and cinnamon. Set aside. Cream the butter and sugar and beat until the mixture is light and fluffy. Beat together the eggs and vanilla, then gradually stir into the butter mixture with the lemon rind. Stir in the flour mixture. Divide the dough into four parts, then roll each into 2-inch diameter logs. Wrap in foil and chill until firm. Preheat the oven to 375°F. Grease two cookie sheets. Cut the dough into ¼-inch slices. Place the rounds on the sheets and bake until lightly colored, about 10 minutes. Transfer to a rack to cool.

INDEX